The
Reference Shelf®

The South China Sea Conflict

The Reference Shelf
Volume 90 • Number 1
H.W. Wilson
A Division of EBSCO Information Services, Inc.

Published by
GREY HOUSE PUBLISHING
Amenia, New York
2018

The Reference Shelf

The books in this series contain reprints of articles, excerpts from books, addresses on current issues, and studies of social trends in the United States and other countries. There are six separately bound numbers in each volume, all of which are usually published in the same calendar year. Numbers one through five are each devoted to a single subject, providing background information and discussion from various points of view and concluding with an index and comprehensive bibliography that lists books, pamphlets, and articles on the subject. The final number of each volume is a collection of recent speeches. Books in the series may be purchased individually or on subscription.

Publisher's Cataloging-In-Publication Data
(Prepared by The Donohue Group, Inc.)

Names: H.W. Wilson Company, compiler.
Title: South China Sea / [compiled by] H. W. Wilson, a division of EBSCO Information
    Services.
Other Titles: Reference shelf ; v. 90, no. 1.
Description: [First edition]. | Amenia, New York : Grey House Publishing, 2018. | Includes
    bibliographical references and index.
Identifiers: ISBN 9781682178645 (v.90, no.1) | ISBN 9781682177471 (volume set)
Subjects: LCSH: South China Sea--Boundaries--Sources. | Territorial waters--Southeast
    Asia. | Trade routes--South China Sea--Sources. | China--Foreign relations--Southeast
    Asia--Sources. | Southeast Asia--Foreign relations--China--Sources.
Classification: LCC KZA1692 .S68 2018 | DDC 341.4/480916472--dc23

Printed in Canada

Contents

1

The Conflict

2

Territorial Disputes and the Law

3

Competing Claims

4

Environmental Concerns

5

Diplomacy, Deterrence and Freedom of Navigation

6

Sovereignty and Codes of Conduct

1
The Conflict

A map of the area of conflict in the South China Sea showing China's nine-dash line.

The South China Sea: An Overview

At its heart, the South China Sea controversy is a territorial dispute. The South China Sea is part of the Pacific Ocean, covering some 3,500,000 square kilometers between the Malacca Straits and the Strait of Taiwan. The sea receives waters from some of the world's most economically important rivers, including the Mekong, the Pampanga, and the Red River, and has served as an important fishing and transportation hub for human societies stretching back thousands of years. In the modern world, the South China Sea carries 80 percent of global trade, thus constituting an essential global economic resource that is vital to the economies of Southeast Asia.[1] On an environmental level, the islands, cays, shoals, atolls, and seamounts, of the South China Sea are one of the most diverse oceanic environments anywhere in the world, making up an important reserve of biodiversity that is currently under a severe threat from overdevelopment and irresponsible utilization practices.

Nations surrounding the South China Sea have been disputing control of the region for centuries and the current controversy can be seen, historically, as a modern iteration of this ancient debate. China has made an historic claim to the vast majority of the sea, based on archaeological data suggesting Chinese settlement on sea islands from at least the Han Dynasty (206 BCE–220 CE). However, Vietnam also has an ancient claim to the region as the nation's Cham ethnic group controlled much of the sea and islands under the long-lived Champa Empire, during which time the South China Sea was known to maritime travelers as the "Champa Sea."[2]

The Roots of the Modern Dispute: Dashed Lines and Warfare

Specialists analyzing the South China Sea conflict typically point to 1947 as the year that the modern phase of the territorial dispute began. That year, marine geographer Yang Huairen, helped create a U-shaped 11-dash line demarcating 90 percent of the South China Sea, which Yang believed, according to his research, was the rightful, sovereign property of China. In a 2016 article in *Time* magazine, Chinese maritime geographer Wang Ying, a disciple of Yang Huairen, explained that the original border was drawn to reflect the location of China's continental shelf as it extends into the sea and that archaeological fragments, including shards of pottery and other artifacts, were used to determine the extent of ancient Chinese imperial settlement in the sea.

Yang used a "dashed line" to reflect the changing nature of marine landscape and as a "humanitarian gesture," reflecting the belief that ships should be allowed to pass through the line freely. In 1952, through a set of political alliances, China ceded control of the Gulf of Tonkin to Vietnam, and this resulted in the loss of two of the original eleven "dashes" in the Chinese territorial claim, thus resulting in the modern "nine-dash line" that the Chinese government uses to express their territorial claim to the sea.[3]

For many years, the Chinese government paid little attention to the islands of the South China Sea, though never relinquishing their official position to ownership of the territory within their theoretical nine-dash line. International conventions and treaties resulted in a patchwork treaty designating the South China Sea as part of international waters and thus, as the nation had no need to fight for access, the issue was considered largely unimportant.

The Law of the Sea

In 1958, United Nations member countries held the United Nations Conference on the Law of the Sea (UNCLOS I), a series of meetings to determine UN international law with regard to maritime disputes. The goals of the convention included developing a legal framework that preserved the right to navigate the ocean for all nations, and to provide a way to manage natural resources on an international scale. Another series of meetings was held in Geneva in 1974, and finally in Jamaica in 1982.

The UNCLOS (versions I, II, and III) meetings collectively resulted in a treaty document, including 320 articles, and 9 annexes that lays out the basic rights for nations to control coastal waters surrounding their sovereign territories. One of the basic principles of UNCLOS is to maintain humanitarian access to the seas for all nations, whether or not the nation is coastal, as part of the shared heritage and resources of humankind.

UNCLOS laws regarding control of the oceans is based on the idea of territorial waters and open, or international waters. The designation is based on the distance from a "baseline," which is typically the low water line on a beach or shore of a continent, or sovereign island. Water that sits on the landward side of a coast is called "inland water," and belongs exclusively to the nation in which the waters sit. This includes, bays, rivers, lakes, and inland seas. From the baselines to 12 miles from the coast is called a "territorial sea," and, within this area, coastal states have the right to establish customs, immigration, sanitation, and navigational laws regarding use of the waters. However, unlike inland waters, no UN member country may prevent "innocent passage," in which a vessel passes through a territory without affecting the peace or security of a coastal nation, in territorial seas. States *are* allowed to temporarily restrict innocent passage through territorial waters, but such restrictions must be announced ahead of time and must be temporary and tied to a just cause under UNCLOS law. The law *does* provide states the right to restrict air passage over territorial waters.

Coastal states may also claim a "contiguous zone," extending another 12 nautical miles from the nation's coast, in which the state has the right to control customs, immigration, and sanitation laws, but may not impose any other travel restrictions, whether by sea or by air. From this boundary, 24 miles from a nation's coast, to 200 miles from the nation's coast, is an area called the "exclusive economic zone" or EEZ. Coastal nations are allowed exclusive rights to develop within this area, controlling all included fisheries, oil, and mineral resources located within their EEZ, but cannot restrict passage through the EEZ to any other nation. Thus, any nation may pass through another nation's EEZ, but may not engage in commercial harvesting or development.

Another important part of UNCLOS that relates to the South China Sea conflict is the definition of an island as a "naturally formed area of land, surrounded by water, which is above water at high tide." If an island falls within a nation's territorial sea, it constitutes a new point for the establishment of the nation's baseline, with the territorial sea extending 12 miles from the coast of the island, rather than from the continental coastline. Islands occurring outside of a nation's territorial sea do not, however, constitute a new baseline. Artificial islands, created by dredging the seafloor to add to an existing rock or other oceanic feature, also do not, according to UNCLOS, provide a nation with a new territorial limit or baseline.[4]

Chinese Expansion

The South China Sea contains three archipelagos, which are groups of islands, but the two most important and most contested of these are the Spratly Islands and the Paracel Islands. China first claimed ownership of the Spratly Islands in 1946 and, 1974, coming the year after the Paris Peace Accords ended the Vietnam Conflict, China invaded the Vietnamese-controlled Paracel Islands. In a two-day skirmish, the Republic of Vietnam Navy was quickly defeated by Chinese forces and forced to retreat. This was the first Sino-Vietnamese skirmish over control of South China Sea territory, and the conflict between the two nations would define the territorial dispute into the twentieth-first century. In 1988, with the area still in dispute, the Chinese again fought South Vietnam for control of the Spratly Islands, with China emerging victorious and establishing military bases on several of the larger islands in the chain.[5]

It has been noted that a 1991 volcanic eruption in the Philippines played a major role in the evolving dispute, forcing the closure of key settlements on some of the sea's islands and leaving room for China to slowly increase its territory. The 1990s then saw an increasing conflict between the Philippines and China for control of parts of the Spratly Islands. In 1995, China occupied Mischief Reef in the Spratlys, located 130 miles from the coast of the Philippines, and some 700 miles from China's nearest island territory, Hainan. China's occupation of Mischief Reef drew international criticism as the feature lies within the EEZ of the Philippines, leading some critics to accuse China of invading territory rightfully controlled by the Philippines.[6]

The South China Sea in the Twenty-First Century

In 2009, China published a new official map in which the government officially staked its claim to all of the territory within the nine-dash line. The claim was immediately controversial, sparking a diplomatic dispute with Vietnam, the Philippines, and the United Nations. In 2011, then Secretary of State Hillary Clinton issued a diplomatic rebuke of China's military policy in the sea, resulting in a U.S. Senate resolution against Chinese South China Sea policy. This came amidst increasing threats between China and Vietnam, and marked a major change in US policy. In July of 2011, the United States and Vietnam engaged in joint naval drills in the region, in a symbolic gesture meant to demonstrate solidarity and encourage international meetings to resolve the issue.[7]

That same year, Exxon Mobil discovered vast oceanic oil deposits off the coast of Vietnam, in a part of the sea lying within China's nine-dash line. In December of 2011, China launched the first aircraft carrier into the disputed territory. The following year, the United States announced at a conference of Asian nations that the United States planned to station at least 60 percent of the nation's naval forces in the Pacific by 2020, helping to reinforce international law. This, the United States announced, would be part of a broad strategy of partnerships with India and Vietnam, to offset China's growing military power in the region.[8]

In 2013, the Philippines announced its intention to arbitrate the dispute within the UN, while China refused to participate. In November of that year, China made a bold move, announcing the establishment of an Air Defense Identification Zone (ADIZ) in the East China Sea, essentially claiming the right to regulate air traffic over much of the nine-dash line territory. The United States, in response, flew jets through the disputed airspace in a display of defiance, drawing criticism from China.

Politics, Diplomacy, Sovereignty

China is a UN member country and a UNCLOS signatory, and yet, most of the nation's territorial claims in the South China Sea are inconsistent with UNCLOS provisions according to international observers and analysts. China, however, disputes this and holds that all of the nation's territorial claims are consistent with UNCLOS. Many of China's claims are not based on interpretation of UNCLOS, but, instead, on contested assertions of sovereignty regarding islands and reefs within the sea. Objections to China's claims in the South China Sea have come primarily from other coastal nations dependent on the sea for shipping or their livelihood. The validity of historic claims to island territories also remains a central component, with as many as five different nations jointly claiming ownership of some of the sea's islands and reefs. In addition to counterterritorial claims, many of the other major objections to China's claims on the region concern humanitarian access to the oceans and freedom of navigation (FON). In addition, while China, Japan, and the United States are major world powers, exerting a powerful military and economic influence on the global community, many of the other nations involved are unable to use military or economic threats to bolster their claims. As the United States and other UN nations increasingly take an interest in the conflict, therefore, the South China debate has taken on elements of a proxy conflict, with the dominant powers manipulating and supporting smaller states as part of a broader struggle for global economic dominance.

Micah L. Issitt

Works Used

Beech, Hannah. "Just Where Exactly Did China Get the South China Sea Nine-Dash Line From?" *Time*. Time, Inc. Jul 19 2016. Web. 15 Nov 2017.

Bray, Adam. "The Cham: Descendants of Ancient Rulers of South China Sea Watch Maritime Dispute from Sidelines." *National Geographic*. National Geographic Society, LLC. Jun 18 2014. Web. 15 Dec 2017.

Hodges, Doyle. "Back to Basics in the South China Sea." *Lawfare*. The Lawfare Institute. Apr 13 2016. Web. 15 Nov 2017.

"How Much Trade Transits the South China Sea?" *China Power*. Center for Strategic & International Studies. Aug 2 2017. Web. 15 Dec 2017.

Pham, Nga. "Shift as Vietnam Marks South China Sea Battle." *BBC*. BBC News. Jan 15 2014. Web. 15 Nov 2017.

Shenon, Philip. "Manila Sees China Threat on Coral Reef." *The New York Times*. The New York Times Co. Feb 19 1995. Web. 15 Nov 2017.

Wan, William. "In South China Sea, Every Side Has Its Say." *The Washington Post*. The Washington Post Co. Jun 20 2011. Web. 15 Nov 2017.

Wan, William. "Panetta, in Speech in Singapore, Seeks to Lend Heft to U.S. Pivot to Asia." *The Washington Post*. The Washington Post, Co. Jun 1 2012. Web. 15 Nov 2017.

Notes

1. "How Much Trade Transits the South China Sea?" *China Power*.
2. Bray, "The Cham: Descendants of Ancient Rulers from South China Sea Watch Maritime Dispute from Sidelines."
3. Beech, "Just Where Exactly Did China Get the South China Sea Nine-Dash Line From?"
4. Hodges, "Back to Basics in the South China Sea."
5. Pham, "Shift as Vietnam Marks South China Sea Battle."
6. Shenon, "Manila Sees China Threat on Coral Reef."
7. Wan, "In South China Sea, Every Side Has Its Say."
8. Wan, "Panetta, in Speech in Singapore, Seeks to Lend Heft to U.S. Pivot to Asia."

China's Biggest Ally in the South China Sea? A Volcano in the Philippines

By Steve Mollman
Quartz, July 10, 2017

On June 15, 1991, an otherwise unremarkable mountain in the Philippines blew its top. And with that massive eruption, Mount Pinatubo became an unlikely actor that profoundly shaped today's South China Sea power contest.

Right in the line of fire of the volcanic eruption, just 9 miles (14.5 km) away, was Clark Air Base, then the most populated overseas US military installation in the world. Also nearby, about 20 miles distant, was the Subic Bay Naval Base.

Together, these sprawling bases, with a combined population exceeding 30,000, had allowed the US to project power in the region. Just by their presence, they made would-be bullies think twice before getting too aggressive. Both bases suffered major damage from the eruption, and by the end of the following year, the US had abandoned them. Ever since, China has slowly been filling the power vacuum that withdrawal created in the South China Sea.

Erupting onto the Scene

British author Simon Winchester, in his 2015 book *Pacific*, devotes a chapter to the eruption's major geopolitical impact. He describes the havoc wreaked upon the bases, noting it was compounded by Typhoon Yunya, which struck the Philippines at the same time:

> The cannonade of millions of tons of ejected material from Pinatubo was believed to have shot twenty miles into the sky, but no one could see the spectacle because of the thick rain clouds and the swirling thunderstorms. All they saw were lightning storms of an unimaginable intensity, and then thousands of tons of liquid ash pouring down on top of everyone and everything for the entire day, collapsing buildings, making roads impassable, turning rivers into torrents of near-solid mud… the two bases below had been wrecked, utterly. They were covered in a foot and more of heavy, gray, and greasy mud. It would take millions of dollars to clean up the bases, and they would be inoperable for years.

Not that Pinatubo went off without a warning. While it caused destruction, it politely gave fair warning before doing so. In March 1991, steam vents began appearing along its ridge, and small tremors were picked up by the US Geological Survey. On June 7, an ash cloud mushroomed into [the] sky, and the Philippine government gave its official warning. Finally, on June 15, Mount Pinatubo erupted.

The fair warning enabled US personnel to leave Clark in an orderly fashion. They headed to Subic, where warships prepared to ferry them away.

The eruption played a direct role in the closing of Clark. The US estimated at the time it would cost over $500 million to make the base operational again. Dick Cheney, then the US defense secretary under president George H.W. Bush, announced in July that Clark was so badly damaged that American forces would abandon it. They did so by November 1991.

The eruption was not the only thing working against the bases. So were US efforts to cut spending and rising nationalism among Philippine politicians. In his 2015 book *Asia's New Battlefield*, Philippine author Richard Javad Heydarian describes the mood in Manila at the time:

> But with the collapse of the USSR in 1991, there was an upsurge of nationalist sentiments, with leading legislators calling for an end to American bases in the Philippines...
> The decisive defeat of communism—long seen as a major threat to Philippine democracy—created a sense of complacency among Filipino leaders.

Such sentiments led to the Americans being kicked off Subic about a year after they left Clark, despite some US hopes that Subic might be spruced up and reoccupied.

Eventually, the US would have left the Philippines anyway. It just would have happened much more slowly. As the *New York Times* noted at the time:

> How the Administration's expectations of a long, phased Philippine withdrawal collapsed into a hasty retreat from two of its largest and oldest overseas bases is the result of an unusual combination of events, including the eruption of a volcano, the demise of the Soviet Union, an assertion of Philippine nationalism, and shrinking Pentagon budgets.

China Makes Its Move

For Beijing, the eruption and US base closings were good news for its South China Sea ambitions. As Winchester notes:

> For the first time in a hundred years, there were no Americans at any base in the Philippines... The island republic... was now essentially defenseless... Overnight, the western Pacific had become a vacuum. One that the Chinese military was only too ready to fill.

In a behavior pattern that has continued until this day, China began taking small, incremental steps to gain a better strategic position in the waterway, as if using the sea for a giant game of Go. In February 1992, Beijing announced that it considered most of the South China Sea its own territory, putting forth its "Law on the Territorial Waters and Their Contiguous Areas."

Soon after it began to build military facilities atop Mischief Reef, a formation of reefs in the Spratlys some 250 km (155) miles from a Philippine coast. In January 1995, local Philippine

> **In a behavior pattern that has continued until this day, China began taking small, incremental steps to gain a better strategic position in the waterway, as if using the sea for a giant game of Go.**

fishermen were surprised to come across huts and platforms arising from the shallows behind the reefs. They were even more surprised when Chinese forces apprehended them on charges of trespassing—even though they were well within the exclusive economic zone of the Philippines.

A diplomatic squabble soon broke out, with Manila summoning the Chinese ambassador for an explanation and China contending it was merely making huts for fishermen, which no one believed. Satellite photos taken over the subsequent years reveal Beijing's true intent: One small step at a time, China turned Mischief Reef into an artificial island, upon which it installed a military base. It did the same to other nearby reefs.

Beijing has insisted that everything within its "nine-dash line"—a crude outline drawn on a map after World War II encompassing most of the sea—is its territory, even though that clashes with modern maritime law and the UN Convention on the Law of the Sea (Unclos).

China has continued with its "salami slicing" strategy—never cutting off a piece big enough to provoke a reaction from its neighbors or the US. There have, though, been occasional flareups. In 2012 China took over Scarborough Shoal, just 200 km (124 miles) from Subic Bay, after a standoff with Philippine forces. And China accelerated its building activity in the Spratlys after the Philippines took its complaints to an international tribunal in 2013. As Beijing feared, the tribunal's highly publicized decision, issued under Unclos in July 2016, discredited China's claims, and found many of its activities in the sea illegal. China scrambled to find other nations to take its side on the issue, with limited success.

By the time of the ruling, which was seen as a big victory for the Philippines, Rodrigo Duterte had just become president. He gave the ruling a shrug and has taken a far more conciliatory—or as some argue defeatist—stance toward China's moves in the South China Sea. He's been more interested in the financing Beijing has offered for big infrastructure projects, though some fear it will lead the Philippines into a debt trap. Among the projects on the table are ones that would touch the former US installations, including a rail link connecting Clark and Subic, and industrial park at Clark.

Beijing is playing the long game in the South China Sea. It knows that flareups die down, that media attention is a fickle thing liable to blow away upon the sea breeze, and that you have to be ready to push forward when an unforeseen opening presents itself. Like that time, a quarter century ago, when a Philippine volcano unexpectedly gave it a hand.

Print Citations

CMS: Mollman, Steve. "China's Biggest Ally in the South China Sea? A Volcano in the Philippines." In *The Reference Shelf: The South China Sea Conflict*, edited by Betsy Maury, 9-12. Ipswich, MA: H.W. Wilson, 2018.

MLA: Mollman, Steve. "China's Biggest Ally in the South China Sea? A Volcano in the Philippines." In *The Reference Shelf: The South China Sea Conflict*. Ed. Betsy Maury. Ipswich: H.W. Wilson, 2018. 9-12. Print.

APA: Mollman, S. (2018). China's biggest ally in the South China Sea? A volcano in the Philippines. In Betsy Maury (Ed.), *The reference shelf: The South China Sea conflict* (pp. 9-12). Ipswich, MA: H.W. Wilson. (Original work published 2017)

The South China Sea Dispute

By Sean Mirski
Lawfare, June 8, 2015

Part I—A Brief History

A small outcropping of sand occasionally breaks the vast expanse of the South China Sea. These islands are modest, even diminutive, but they form the core of a fierce territorial dispute among six primary claimants: Brunei, China, Malaysia, the Philippines, Taiwan, and Vietnam. These claimants also clash over their rights and duties in the nearby waters as well as the seabed underneath.

The disputes in the South China Sea have the potential to ignite a broader regional conflagration. Multiple claimants contend over issues of sovereignty not susceptible to easy legal resolution. Worse, the stakes are high: the Sea is one of the primary routes for international trade, and many claimants believe that the Sea hides bountiful oil reserves in addition to its plentiful fishing stocks. The disputes are further entrenched by rampant nationalism, as each claimant attaches symbolic value to the South China Sea islands that far exceeds their objective material wealth. And, finally, the disputes are also tinged by great power politics as China and the United States begin to jostle each other for control of the international order.

Over the last year, disputes in the South China Sea have dominated headlines, and they seem sure to continue to generate fresh national security issues. Already, too, they have raised a variety of legal questions that will inform the future course of both the conflict and the region.

Accordingly, *Lawfare* decided to prepare a backgrounder on the South China Sea that proceeds in two parts. First, in this part, I will lay out the history of the disputes and highlight key events necessary to understanding the crises of the day. In the second part, I will introduce the primary legal issues underlying the disputes.

Centuries of Contested History

The islands of the South China Sea can largely be grouped into two island chains. The Paracel Islands are clustered in the northwest corner of the Sea, and the Spratly Islands in the southeast corner.

Reflecting the Rashomon nature of the dispute, the claimants have argued bitterly over the "true" history of these island chains. Some have tried to ground their modern claims by proving a long and unbroken record of national control over claimed features. These states assert that, for example, their nationals fished around the islands of the Sea or used them for shelter from storms. In particular, Beijing has taken an active role in subsidizing archeological digs to find evidence of exclusive Chinese usage of the Sea's many features since time immemorial.

It is hard—if not impossible—to wade through these partisan claims (many of which constitute pure propaganda). No impartial tribunal has yet taken on that challenge. To the extent that it is possible to draw any conclusions from the morass, though, it seems fair to say that no claimant has conclusively demonstrated a pattern of exclusive historical control over the South China Sea, or even over isolated parts of it.

A Period of Relative Quiet

In any case, the issue was moot for most of the region's history. Through the first half of the twentieth century, the Sea remained quiet as neighboring states focused their attention on conflicts unfolding elsewhere.

In fact, at the end of World War II, no claimant occupied a single island in the entire South China Sea. Then, in 1946, China established itself on a few features in the Spratlys, and in early 1947, it also snapped up Woody Island, part of the Paracel Islands chain, only two weeks before the French and Vietnamese intended to make landfall. Denied their first pick, the French and Vietnamese settled for the nearby Pattle Island.

But even at this stage, the South China Sea was not seen as a priority by any of the claimants. For that reason, after suffering their cataclysmic defeat at the hands of Mao's Communists, Chiang Kai-shek's forces retreated to Taiwan and abandoned their stations in the South China Sea. Even the French and Vietnamese could not be bothered to take advantage of the lapse in Chinese control, as they were preoccupied with the rapidly escalating war in Vietnam.

The Claimants Rush for Control

However, the next half century saw accelerating interest in the South China Sea. In 1955 and 1956, China and Taiwan established permanent presences on several key islands, while a Philippine citizen—Thomas Cloma—claimed much of the Spratly Island chain as his own.

Once again, this phase of frenetic island occupation was cooled off by a longer period of inertia. But by the early 1970s, the claimants were at it once again. This time, though, the scramble was spurred by indications that oil lurked beneath the waters of the South China Sea. The Philippines was the first to move. China followed shortly thereafter with a carefully coordinated seaborne invasion of several islands. In the Battle of the Paracel Islands, it wrested several features out from under South Vietnam's control, killing several dozen Vietnamese and sinking a corvette in the process. In response, both South and North Vietnam reinforced their remaining garrisons and seized several other unoccupied features.

Another decade of relative inaction was punctuated once again with violence in 1988, when Beijing moved into the Spratlys and set off another round of occupations by the claimants. Tensions crested when Beijing forcibly occupied Johnson Reef, killing several dozen Vietnamese sailors in the process.

Once again, though, tensions deescalated for a few years, only to rise again in 1995, when Beijing built bunkers above Mischief Reef in the wake of a Philippine oil concession.

Diplomatic Developments

The dispute seemed to take a turn for the better in 2002, when ASEAN and China came together to sign the Declaration on the Conduct of Parties in the South China Sea. The Declaration sought to establish a framework for the eventual negotiation of a Code of Conduct for the South China Sea. The parties promised "to exercise self-restraint in the conduct of

> **The disputes are further entrenched by rampant nationalism, as each claimant attaches symbolic value to the South China Sea islands that far exceeds their objective material wealth.**

activities that would complicate or escalate disputes and affect peace and stability including, among others, refraining from action of inhabiting on the presently uninhabited islands, reefs, shoals, cays, and other features and to handle their differences in a constructive manner."

For a while, the Declaration seemed to keep conflict at bay. Over the next half decade, Beijing launched a charm offensive across Southeast Asia, and the claimants refrained from provoking each other by occupying additional features.

Rather than fighting battles out on the Sea, though, the claimants began to needle each other through demarches and notes verbales. In May 2009, Malaysia and Vietnam sent a joint submission to the Commission on the Limits of the Continental Shelf setting out some of their claims. This initial submission unleashed a flurry of *notes verbales* from the other claimants, who objected to the two nation's claims.

In particular, China responded to the joint submission by submitting a map containing the infamous "nine-dash" line. This line snakes around the edges of the South China Sea and encompasses all of the Sea's territorial features as well as the vast majority of its waters. However, Beijing has never officially clarified what the line is meant to signify. Instead, it has maintained "strategic ambiguity" and said only that "China has indisputable sovereignty over the islands in the South China Sea and the adjacent waters, and enjoys sovereign rights and jurisdiction over the relevant waters as well as the seabed and subsoil thereof (see attached map)." This could mean that China claims only the territorial features in the Sea and any "adjacent waters" allowed under maritime law. Or it could mean that China claims all the territorial features and all the waters enclosed by the nine-dash line, even those that exceed what's permitted under maritime law.

Recent Crises

Since the publication of the nine-dash line, the region has grown increasingly concerned by China's perceived designs on the South China Sea. In 2012, Beijing bore out some of these concerns when it snatched Scarborough Shoal away from the Philippines. The two states had quarreled over allegations of illegal poaching by Chinese fishermen. After a two-month standoff, the parties agreed to each withdraw from the Shoal. Manila did. Beijing did not. Since then, China has excluded Philippine boats from the Shoal's waters.

In response to this escalatory move, Manila filed an arbitration case against China on January 22, 2013, under the auspices of the U.N. Convention on the Law of the Sea (UNCLOS). The Philippine claims center around maritime law issues, although China asserts that they cannot be resolved without deciding territorial issues first. For that reason, Beijing has largely refused to participate in the proceedings, although it has drafted and publicly released a position paper opposing the tribunal's jurisdiction. The Philippines has submitted its memorial as well as a response to China's position paper, and both nations are currently awaiting a decision from the tribunal as to its own jurisdiction.

As the case proceeds in the background, China has adopted an increasingly assertive posture in the region. In early May 2014, a Chinese state-owned oil company moved one of its rigs into waters claimed by Vietnam south of the Paracel Islands. This provocation touched off confrontations between Vietnamese and Chinese vessels around the rig, as well as rioting against foreign-owned businesses in parts of Vietnam. Faced with this pushback, China withdrew the rig in mid-July, a month ahead of schedule.

Additionally, over the last year, Beijing has launched an accelerating land reclamation campaign across the South China Sea. In at least seven locations, Chinese vessels have poured tons of sand to expand the size of features occupied by China. Beijing has also begun construction of infrastructure on much of this reclaimed land, including an airstrip capable of receiving military aircraft. Although other claimants have reclaimed land in the past, China has reclaimed 2,000 acres of new land, more than "all other claimants combined over the history of their claims," according to the U.S. Department of Defense.

The other claimants have condemned this latest project as counterproductive, and President Obama has urged China to stop "throwing elbows and pushing people out of the way" in pursuit of its interests. Thus far, Beijing has not complied with these entreaties, and it is unclear what the next twist or turn in the story of the South China Sea will be.

Part II—A Legal Primer

Although the United States will often urge the claimants to resolve the South China Sea dispute in accordance with "international law" writ broadly, the conflict is governed in reality by a number of different bodies of international law. Building on the historical backgrounder in an earlier post, I will lay out here the two primary legal quarrels at the core of the South China Sea conflict: the dispute over territory and the dispute over the substance and application of maritime law.

Territorial Dispute

In the South China Sea dispute, the claimants are squabbling first and foremost over sovereignty over the Sea's territorial features. At its most basic, the claimants disagree over who owns each of the features. Some claimants—like Brunei and Malaysia—have advanced relatively modest territorial claims. Others—like the Philippines and especially Vietnam—have asserted ownership over a much larger proportion of the Sea's features. Finally, China (and Taiwan) have laid claim to every piece of territory in the entire Sea. (See picture above for a map of these overlapping claims.)

To back up their claims, the six states have relied on the law of sovereignty. A bit of background: the law of sovereignty is part of customary international law, and it originally prescribed five different methods of acquiring sovereignty over territory. One of those methods—conquest—is no longer consider lawful (Crimea notwithstanding), but it remains potentially relevant as the historical source of authority for some of the disputants' claims. The other four methods continue to be recognized today. States can gain territory through the process of accretion, or the expansion of existing territory through natural processes like volcanic eruptions. States can also transfer sovereignty over territory to each other through the process of cession. If a state discovers and then effectively occupies new territory (known as terra nullius), then it can acquire sovereignty over that unclaimed territory through the process of effective occupation. Finally, a state can gain sovereignty over another state's territory by occupying it publicly, peacefully, and uninterruptedly for a sufficiently long time. This process is called prescription, and it mirrors the doctrine of adverse possession in American property law.

Notably, sovereignty law does not put stock in the proximity of a state to its territorial claims. As I've noted before, the Permanent Court of Arbitration held in the highly influential Island of Palmas case that "it is impossible to show the existence of a rule of positive international law to the effect that islands situated outside territorial waters should belong to a State from the mere fact that its territory forms the terra firma(nearest continent or island of considerable size)." So while it may seem absurd to many that Beijing may have a stronger claim than Manila to an island right off the Philippine coast, that outcome is not foreclosed by the law of sovereignty. (Indeed, consider the case of the United States and Alaska or Hawaii.)

In the South China Sea, the six claimants have mixed and matched sovereignty law's doctrines in order to stitch together legally convincing claims. Some claimants, like China and Vietnam, have tried to unearth a long history of effective occupation by their national predecessors. Vietnam has also tried to justify its ownership by tracing title back to its colonial occupier, France. In contrast, the Philippines has argued that—whatever the history of Chinese and Vietnamese use—the Spratly Islands were abandoned by the time that Philippine citizen Thomas Cloma stumbled upon them in the 1950s, and that Cloma was able to acquire and then transfer

> **Whereas sovereignty law governs who may exert full sovereignty over the territorial features of the South China Sea, maritime law governs what jurisdiction states may exert over the nearby waters and the seabed underneath.**

sovereignty over them to the Philippines.

Sifting through these claims is a Herculean task, and one that may prove impossible in the end. Indeed, after surveying the available evidence, Bill Hayton argues that the legal question itself makes no conceptual sense—the Western idea of "sovereignty" or "ownership" simply does not translate into the historical context of the South China Sea, where sovereignty was often overlapping, graduated, or patchy. As a result, "[i]n no sense did any state or people 'own' the Sea."

In any event, the claimants have shown little appetite thus far for handing over the territorial issues in the South China Sea dispute to an impartial tribunal, perhaps because no claimant is especially confident in their legal justifications. As a result, the territorial issue seems most likely to be resolved ultimately on the basis of a political settlement rather than a legal ruling.

The parties are far from beginning serious negotiations on this score, however. China insists on bilateral negotiations, while the smaller claimants favor multilateral talks where they can band together to counteract their northern neighbor's heft. For now, then, the legal issue is likely to remain overshadowed by changing events on the ground.

Maritime Dispute

Alongside the territorial dispute, the claimants have also clashed over issues related to maritime law. Whereas sovereignty law governs who may exert full sovereignty over the territorial features of the South China Sea, maritime law governs what jurisdiction states may exert over the nearby waters and the seabed underneath. So, for instance, the United States has sovereignty over the territory of Hawaii, but it is maritime law that decides the extent of its offshore jurisdiction. Because maritime law reaches beyond the disputed territories, it has pulled a variety of other parties into the vortex of the South China Sea dispute (including Indonesia and the United States).

Maritime law has largely been codified in the U.N. Convention on the Law of the Sea (UNCLOS). The vast majority of nations have ratified UNCLOS, including all the primary claimants in the South China Sea dispute. While the treaty has not yet been ratified by the United States, Washington has made clear that it sees most of the treaty's substantive provisions as reflecting customary international law binding on allcountries.

Yet despite the high degree of consensus surrounding UNCLOS, there are several statutory ambiguities or gaps that have precipitated contested interpretations by the claimants.

To begin with, the claimants disagree about the scope of jurisdiction that UN-CLOS entitles them to over the South China Sea's waters. In particular, the claimants have different views about the boundaries of the various national exclusive economic zones (EEZs) and continental-shelf zones. Part of the disagreement stems from the territorial dispute—maritime zones are drawn from a territorial baseline, so without agreement over that baseline, states will disagree about the size and shape of the zones. But the disagreement also stems from differences of opinion about how UNCLOS classifies each of the territorial features. Under UNCLOS, certain territorial features are entitled to greater maritime zones than others, as I've explained in greater depth before. So for example, if a feature (1) surfaces above the ocean at high tide, and (2) can "sustain human habitation or economic life of [its] own," then it is entitled to a 200-nautical-mile EEZ, in which the sovereign may "explor[e] and exploit[], conserv[e] and manag[e] the natural resources, whether living or non-living, of the waters superjacent to the seabed and of the seabed and its subsoil," among other rights. Because the claimants disagree over how to classify the territorial features of the South China Sea (for instance, whether they can sustain human habitation or economic life of their own), they also disagree about the scope and type of the attached maritime zones.

Many of these issues are playing out in the Philippines's arbitration case against China. In January 2013, Manila sued China for breaching the provisions of UN-CLOS. In its case, the Philippines is making three primary claims, all related to maritime jurisdiction: first, that Beijing claims more of the South China Sea's waters than the Convention permits; second, and relatedly, that China has claimed 200-nautical-mile EEZs for a number of insular features not entitled to them; and third, that China has violated other rights guaranteed to the Philippines by UN-CLOS. Right now, the tribunal is still deciding on its own jurisdiction to hear the case—Beijing argues that the maritime issues are too entwined with the territorial ones to be capable of resolution on their own—but if the court moves to the merits, then it may deal a serious blow to China's maritime claims as encapsulated in the infamous nine-dash line.

Besides quarrels over the scope of EEZs and the like, the South China Sea parties also feud over the rights that states have within those maritime zones. In particular, the United States and China have offered competing interpretations of the lawfulness of foreign military activities in another country's EEZ. Relying on a variety of UNCLOS provisions and security-based arguments, Beijing contends that these "hostile" activities breach the letter and spirit of the Convention. The United States disagrees. According to it, military activities in another country's EEZ are supported by a long history of state practice, and nothing in the Convention purports to prohibit them. (Beijing may be warming to this view—recently, it collected intelligence in the United States's EEZ—but it has not officially altered its views yet.) This interpretational difference has provoked crises in the past: the American military often collects intelligence in China's EEZ, and Beijing has occasionally tried to interfere with those activities—sometimes with serious consequences.

None of these legal issues is likely to disappear any time soon. The underlying drivers of the conflict are simply too powerful to let the legal issues be resolved without some parallel political compromise. Nevertheless, the legal issues continue to frame the dispute in important ways, and must be dealt with on the way to any long-term solution.

Print Citations

CMS: Mirski, Sean. "The South China Sea Dispute." In *The Reference Shelf: The South China Sea Conflict*, edited by Betsy Maury, 13-20. Ipswich, MA: H.W. Wilson, 2018.

MLA: Mirski, Sean. "The South China Sea Dispute." In *The Reference Shelf: The South China Sea Conflict*. Ed. Betsy Maury. Ipswich: H.W. Wilson, 2018. 13-20. Print.

APA: Mirski, S. (2018). The South China Sea Dispute. In Betsy Maury (Ed.), *The reference shelf: The South China Sea conflict* (pp. 13-20). Ipswich, MA: H.W. Wilson. (Original work published 2015)

China v the Rest

The Economist, March 26, 2016

For years China has sought to divide and rule in the South China Sea. It worked hard to prevent the countries challenging it over some or all of its absurdly aggrandising territorial claims in the sea from ganging up against it. So when tensions with one rival claimant were high, it tended not to provoke others.

Not any more. In a kind of united-front policy in reverse, it now seems content to antagonise them all at the same time. This is both encouraging closer co-operation among neighbours and driving them closer to external powers including India, Australia, Japan and, above all, America.

The latest fight China has picked is with a country with which—unlike Brunei, Malaysia, the Philippines, Taiwan and Vietnam—it has no territorial dispute: Indonesia. On March 21st the chargé d'affaires at China's embassy in Jakarta was hauled in to receive a stiff protest. A Chinese coastguard vessel had rammed free a Chinese fishing boat as it was towed into port after being caught allegedly fishing in Indonesian waters. The crew of eight was already in detention. In a similar incident three years ago, Indonesia released detained crew members when confronted by an armed "maritime law-enforcement" vessel belonging to China's fisheries bureau.

Since that incident Indonesia has elected a new president, Joko Widodo, one of whose trumpeted policies has been to look after the interests of fishermen. To deter illegal interlopers, Indonesia now impounds and blows up foreign vessels caught poaching. In this case, it seems clear that the Chinese were in Indonesian waters. Indonesia claims that the boat was just four kilometres off the Natuna islands, well within Indonesia's 12 nautical-mile territorial limit, let alone its 200-nautical-mile "exclusive economic zone" (EEZ).

China explicitly acknowledges Indonesian sovereignty over the Natunas. Yet instead of apologising, China's foreign ministry demanded the fishermen's release, claiming that they had been carrying out "normal operations" in "traditional Chinese fishing grounds". China is a party to the UN Convention on the Law of the Sea (UNCLOS), under which countries are entitled to territorial waters and EEZs. Yet the government's implicit argument is that a self-proclaimed "tradition" trumps international law. By extension, with 5,000 years of sacred history touted ad nauseam by its Communist Party leaders, who is to deny China anything it wants?

China's tradition-based argument also has implications for its "nine-dash line" delimiting its claim to virtually all of the South China Sea (and passing just north of the Natunas). It would suggest China believes it has rights over not just land features inside the line, and their territorial seas and EEZs, but also over all the water itself—a concept alien to UNCLOS.

Flaky Claims, Fake Islands

China has declined to explain how its claims fit within UNCLOS parameters. Indeed it has a record of flouting the law and international agreements when it comes to the sea. In 2002 it signed a joint declaration with the ten-member Association of South-East Asian Nations, in which the parties undertook to "exercise self-restraint" in the South China Sea, and in particular to refrain from occupying uninhabited features such as reefs. That commitment is hard to square with the massive building spree on which China has been engaged for the past two years in the Spratly archipelago, turning seven uninhabitable rocks and reefs submerged at high tide into artificial islands. Vietnam and the Philippines, rival claimants, have naturally been outraged. And this month an American admiral has reported Chinese activity at Scarborough Shoal, north of the Spratlys, that suggests it might be the "next possible area of reclamation". China bullied the Philippines away from the shoal four years ago.

> China is a party to the UN Convention of the Law of the Sea (UNCLOS), under which countries are entitled to territorial waters and EEZs. Yet the government's implicit argument is that a self-proclaimed "tradition" trumps international law.

The Philippines has asked an international tribunal, the Permanent Court of Arbitration in The Hague, to rule on some of China's claims under UNCLOS. The court is expected to announce its verdict soon. If it rules broadly in favour of the Philippines, it would have the effect of making clear that China's nine-dash line has no legal basis. China is boycotting the case and says it will ignore the verdict. The ruling might embarrass China. But it will not stop it creating artificial islands, or indeed make it dismantle those it has already built.

It seems increasingly likely that the islands will have a military purpose. China denies that, but it is hard to see why else it needs the long airstrip it is building on the Fiery Cross reef in the Spratlys. It is in this context that the threat of building at Scarborough Shoal causes such alarm. China has controlled the whole of the Paracel chain in the north of the South China Sea since 1974, when it drove out the former South Vietnamese from part of it. It has recently installed missile batteries on Woody Island there. In the Spratlys to the south it is building what look like potential air and naval bases, complete with military-grade radars. Scarborough Shoal would complete a "strategic triangle" that would allow it to dominate the sea. China is widely expected one day to declare an "air defence identification zone" over the sea, as it has over parts of the East China Sea, including areas contested with Japan.

Aggressors rarely see themselves as such. Indeed China accuses the United States of being the driving force behind the "militarisation" of the sea. Certainly America is responding to Chinese moves. Last year it resumed naval "freedom of navigation" operations, sending warships close to disputed features. This month it sent an aircraft-carrier strike group into the sea. American naval and marine-corps commanders have been in Vietnam to explore co-operation. Worse, from China's viewpoint, American forces have just obtained access to five Philippine bases, including an airbase on Palawan, just opposite the Spratlys. For this, China's official news agency accused America of "muddying the waters" and "making the Asia-Pacific a second Middle East".

China will not be deterred, confident that America is unlikely to risk a serious crisis, let alone conflict. China's throwing its weight around in the sea erodes America's credibility as the pre-eminent military power in the western Pacific, but does not directly threaten it. By contrast, rather than cow China, America's enhanced military role gives it a pretext to carry on with its build-up. There is still the danger, however, of an accidental flare-up—a skirmish over illegal fishing, for example, and an ensuing escalation. Armed conflict in the South China Sea is a long way from being inevitable. But it is far from unthinkable.

Print Citations

CMS: "China v the Rest." In *The Reference Shelf: The South China Sea Conflict*, edited by Betsy Maury, 21-23. Ipswich, MA: H.W. Wilson, 2018.

MLA: "China v the Rest." *The Reference Shelf: The South China Sea Conflict*. Ed. Betsy Maury. Ipswich: H.W. Wilson, 2018. 21-23. Print.

APA: The Economist. (2018). China v the rest. In Betsy Maury (Ed.), *The reference shelf: The South China Sea conflict* (pp. 21-23). Ipswich, MA: H.W. Wilson. (Original work published 2016)

The South China Sea—Some Fundamental Strategic Principles

By Amy Searight and Geoffrey Hartman
Center for Strategic & International Studies, **January 26, 2017**

A critical and early Chinese test of U.S. resolve is likely to come in the South China Sea, where Washington has struggled to respond effectively to assertive Chinese behavior. Enduring U.S. interests—freedom of navigation and overflight, support for the rules-based international order, and the peaceful resolution of disputes—are at risk in the region. U.S. goals to uphold regional alliances and partnerships, defend international rules and norms, and maintain a productive relationship with China remain valid. China has seized the initiative in the South China Sea, however, and the United States needs to revamp its strategy to reverse current trends and escape the trap of reactive and ineffectual policymaking. To this end, the new administration should perform an early, top-down, and thorough strategic review to enable greater consistency and effectiveness in U.S. South China Sea policy.

China is undertaking a persistent, long-term effort to establish control over the South China Sea. Under President Xi Jinping, Beijing has undertaken more assertive policies that have greatly improved Beijing's position in the South China Sea. China remains uncompromising on sovereignty, has increased its capability to enforce its de facto control in disputed areas, and has sought to advance its claims while staying below the threshold for direct military conflict with the United States.

- China has steadily built capabilities and infrastructure, most notably military facilities on artificial islands, that enable greater control of the South China Sea. The growing size and capability of the Chinese air force, navy, and coast guard allow Beijing to consistently monitor and exercise de facto control over most of the South China Sea. China's island outposts will increase this advantage as Chinese aircraft, ships, and paramilitary vessels will be able to rest and resupply in the southern portion of the South China Sea.

- China is already providing indications of how it might act when it controls the South China Sea. China has harassed U.S. Navy ships operating in the South China Sea, warned military flights to stay away from its artificial islands, and recently seized a U.S. drone operating in the exclusive economic zone of the Philippines. These actions suggest that China might undermine freedom of navigation and overflight, principles of fundamental importance to the United States.

- China has shown it is willing to accept substantial risk to achieve its ends, and has engaged in outright coercion against weaker neighbors like the Philippines and Vietnam. U.S. allies and partners in the region are drawing lessons from Chinese coercive behavior and the limited U.S. response to it, and some are beginning to doubt U.S. resolve and adjust their foreign policies in response.

U.S. responses to China's South China Sea activities have been insufficient to alter China's behavior and have fed the narrative that China is pushing the United States out of the region. Countering China's efforts has become a key test of perceived U.S. commitment to many in the region. If Chinese coercion goes unchallenged by the United States, it will send a dangerous signal about the strength of the U.S. alliance system and lessen the appeal of the United States as a security partner.

- The United States has been largely successful at preserving its own freedom of action and deterring outright Chinese aggression in the South China Sea through routine presence operations. U.S. access to the South China Sea is coming under increasing threat as Chinese power increases, but can be preserved if the United States maintains a sufficient military advantage over China.

- The United States has been less successful in supporting local partners as they resist Chinese coercion. The United States has an interest in seeing that these partners maintain their strategic autonomy, but capacity building efforts to help them resist coercion are not keeping pace with China's growing capabilities. This puts more pressure on Washington to intervene and U.S. allies and partners in Asia are watching carefully and drawing conclusions about U.S. commitment and staying power in the region.

- The United States also faces a challenge in enforcing international law in the South China Sea. U.S. military advantage is of limited utility in this area and Washington has struggled to convince local partners to join in freedom of navigation operations. The United States needs to consider a wider variety of non-military responses to China's efforts to control the South China Sea, and more effectively build a local coalition to support these responses.

To counter China's efforts to control the South China Sea, the United States needs a sustainable strategy to bolster its own capabilities, work more effectively with capable allies and partners, and strengthen the regional order.

- Preserving the U.S. military edge is key to maintaining the U.S. position in Asia. The United States should continue to prioritize military presence in the Asia-Pacific at the same time as it invests in key capabilities, such as long-range precision strike, undersea warfare, cyber/space systems, and other capabilities that will preserve the U.S. ability to deter Chinese aggression.

- The United States can do more to leverage its alliances in Asia to raise the costs of Chinese efforts to undermine the regional order. Allied efforts to support U.S. force posture in the region will remain vital, but the United States should also expect allies to make greater contributions in responding to Chinese coercion. Close allies such as Australia and Japan have a great deal to offer in terms of capability and capacity, and should be encouraged to do more.

Guidelines for a South China Sea Strategy

As the new administration sets out to revamp U.S. strategy in the South China Sea, it should keep the following guidelines in mind:

- **Pursue Deterrence and Cooperation Simultaneously**

  Although Chinese cooperation is necessary to address some regional and global issues—such as North Korea's belligerent behavior and climate change—the United States should not be held hostage by concerns that a more robust deterrence strategy will thwart bilateral cooperation. Any temptation to alter U.S. policies in the South China Sea to preserve cooperation with China in other areas is unnecessary and potentially counterproductive. Cooperation on areas of shared interest is important not only to the United States, but also to China.

  U.S. leaders should not be afraid of tension in the U.S.-China relationship. The United States can stand firm on its principles and deter China from undermining the regional order while maintaining a productive relationship. Giving ground on vital interests in Asia will not encourage greater cooperation on global issues. Instead, perceptions of weakness may encourage leaders in Beijing to embrace more assertive behavior. In short, adopting a more robust deterrence approach need not prevent cooperation that is in the interests of both countries.

- **Adopt Consistent and Sustainable Policies and Messages**

  The new administration should issue clear and consistent strategic messages, since inconsistent articulation of the objectives of the rebalance strategy has caused confusion in China and amongst U.S. allies and partners. In particular, shifting explanations for how the United States will manage China's rising power and influence—along with the military-heavy implementation of the rebalance—have exacerbated suspicions that Washington seeks to contain Beijing's rise.

  Inconsistent messaging and policies—including on freedom of navigation and routine presence operations—have also led to confusion in the region. The new administration should provide authoritative explanations of these operations and not alter their schedule in response to Chinese pressure. Moving forward, freedom of navigation and routine presence operations should be executed on a regular basis to

> **The United States can stand firm on its principles and deter China from undermining the regional order while maintaining a productive relationship.**

demonstrate U.S. resolve to fly, sail, and operate wherever international law allows. While consistency in U.S. messaging and policy execution is important, it should be balanced by carefully calculated unpredictability in operations and tactics to prevent Beijing from becoming overly confident in its ability to anticipate U.S. reactions.

- Expand the Policy Toolkit

U.S. policy in the South China Sea has been overly reliant on military options, which may not always be the most effective response. Diplomatic, informational, legal, and economic responses are currently underrepresented in U.S. China policy, and their incorporation into the policy toolkit will be important for successfully dissuading China over the long-term. For example, targeted sanctions on Chinese companies involved in destabilizing activities could be considered. The United States has leverage over China in areas not directly related to South China Sea and may have to consider using or threatening to use these tools to stabilize the regional order.

- Reinvigorate Engagement with Allies and Partners

The United States should intensify capacity building efforts with allies and partners to improve their ability to resist Chinese coercion. Successful capacity building efforts will allow Southeast Asian states to better help themselves, bolstering deterrence against low-level Chinese coercion and allowing the U.S. military to focus more on deterring high-level contingencies. To facilitate capacity building, Washington should preserve regional defense relationships while recognizing that the ability of the United States to partner with frontline states depends on their cooperation and adherence to good governance and human rights.

The United States has several enduring advantages that make regional states continue to seek it out as the security partner of choice, including the world's best military, high favorability ratings in most local populations, and a less threatening foreign policy than that of China. Given these advantages, Washington can afford to focus on the long game in Asia, confident that Chinese adventurism is likely to push many states to turn to the United States for support.

- Maintain a Principled Position on Disputes

  The longstanding U.S. position that it takes no position on sovereignty disputes over land features in the South China Sea, while insisting that these disputes be resolved in a peaceful fashion and in accordance with international law, is sound and should be maintained.

  This principled stand allows the United States to defend its interests without embroiling itself in the murky sovereignty claims at the heart of the South China Sea dispute. Not taking a position on sovereignty allows the United States to flexibly intervene in the South China Sea to defend its interests and international rules and norms, while undercutting Chinese attempts to paint U.S. actions as a threat to Beijing's sovereignty. Other claimant states welcome U.S. involvement precisely because Washington does not favor one claimant's territorial ambitions over those of the others.

Print Citations

CMS: Searight, Amy, and Geoffrey Hartman. "The South China Sea—Some Fundamental Principles." In *The Reference Shelf: The South China Sea Conflict*, edited by Betsy Maury, 24-28. Ipswich, MA: H.W. Wilson, 2018.

MLA: Searight, Amy, and Geoffrey Hartman. "The South China Sea—Some Fundamental Principles." *The Reference Shelf: The South China Sea Conflict*. Ed. Betsy Maury. Ipswich: H.W. Wilson, 2018. 24-28. Print.

APA: Searight, A., & G. Hartman. (2018). The South China Sea—Some fundamental principles. In Betsy Maury (Ed.), *The reference shelf: The South China Sea conflict* (pp. 24-28). Ipswich, MA: H.W. Wilson. (Original work published 2017)

2

Territorial Disputes and the Law

This photo taken on July 14, 2016 shows Chinese ships putting out a fire on a mock cargo vessel during an emergency drill in the South China Sea near Sansha, in south China's Hainan province. China warned on July 14 of a 'decisive response' to provocations in the South China Sea, as it faced mounting pressure to accept an international tribunal's ruling against its claims to most of the strategically vital waters.

The Legal Dimension: The South China Sea and the Law

The United National Convention on the Law of the Sea (UNCLOS) is a framework of treaties designed to create the basis for negotiation and arbitration involving oceanic territory. As with any body of international agreements, the legality of the treaty and the degree to which nations are required to adhere to the framework, is often unclear. In the South China Sea conflict, China has repeatedly engaged in military and development projects in violation of UNCLOS principles and yet, there remains little consensus on how best to cope with the issue, how to arbitrate between China and other nations with conflicting territorial claims, and how or whether UNCLOS can be enforced as a body of law.

The Basics of United Nations Law

The United Nations began in 1942, in the form of a 26-nation alliance dedicated to fighting the Axis Powers in World War II. The name chosen by Franklin Roosevelt was preserved when, in October of 1945, representatives of 50 nations met in San Francisco, creating what became the official United Nations Charter. The charter, ratified by 51 nations that year, was designed with a specific mission: To avoid another world war and to create a framework for resolving disputes and creating international agreements that helped meet collective goals.[1] Membership in the organization is a privilege that is offered to nations who agree to adhere to basic UN principles on international engagement and human rights and yet, the politics involving membership are complex and not all member nations agree to all of the conventions produced by the organization.

Whether or not a nation adheres to UN conventions on issues like environmental protection, or women's rights, depends largely on whether sitting heads of state or governments see the goals of their nation reflected in the collective principles of the United Nations. On March 21, 2016, for instance, President Donald Trump, in a Tweet, alleged, "The United Nations is not a friend of democracy, it's not a friend to freedom, it's not a friend even to the United States of America ..."[2] Trump's disdain for the organization is predictable, as Trump's policies on immigration, nuclear proliferation, and environmental protection, and the Trump administration's antimulticultural ideology, are at stark odds with the principles and policies of the UN. Similarly, in the South China Sea controversy, China has been deeply critical of the United Nations and has refused to abide by UN conventions regarding maritime boundaries and the ownership of oceanic resources. In some cases, powerful member nations will refuse to ratify conventions on certain controversial issues. For instance, the United States did not ratify the UNCLOS, and so is not bound by the treaty's laws.

In 1899, hundreds of delegates representing 26 countries gathered for the First Peace Conference in the Hague (Den Haag), the third-largest city in the Netherlands. The Hague, long serving as an international city for conferences and meetings, was thus chosen as the official site for international arbitration and legal disputes after the formation of the League of Nations, and later the United Nations.[3] The Permanent Court of Arbitration, a neutral legal body designed specifically to arbitrate disputes between countries, was the first UN court established in the Hague, which also became the site of the International Court of Justice (ICJ), which is the highest international court of the United Nations. In 1998 the UN created the International Criminal Court (ICC), which is convened to hear cases involving genocide, war crimes, and crimes against humanity. The degree to which United Nations member countries agree to adhere to the decisions of UN courts varies. For instance, the United States, Israel, Russia, and China do not recognize the authority of the ICC.[4]

The United Nations courts and tribunals only have power insomuch as nations involved in a dispute agree to adhere to the rulings of the courts. For signatory nations, meaning nations that *have* agreed to recognize the UN courts, failure to adhere to conventions can result in various types of penalties. First, the courts may issue a warrant for the arrest of an individual responsible for a certain international crime. Second, the courts may recommend sanctions to the UN, which are international penalties imposed largely through trade and economic agreements. For instance, in the ongoing controversy regarding nuclear proliferation in North Korea, the United Nations has imposed sanctions that restrict imports and exports to the nation, as well as prohibiting member nations from providing economic support or engaging in commercial activities within the nation. Finally, a nation may be expelled from the UN, which means losing access to many of the treaties, protections, and international trade agreements available to member nations.

The Law of the Sea

The United Nations Convention on the Law of the Sea (UNCLOS) is an international treaty with 167 member states. One of the most important parts of UNCLOS is the determination of how to define a nation's ownership over oceanic resources. UNCLOS thus divides the ocean into "territorial waters," which include all waters from the baseline (the low water line from the furthest coastal territory), to 12 nautical miles. There is also a contiguous zone, extending another 12 nautical miles further from the edge of the territorial zone. Both of these zones sit within a coastal nation's exclusive economic zone (EEZ), which extends 200 miles from the coast and defines an area in which a coastal nation has exclusive access to the mineral and biological resources. According to UNCLOS, all oceanic waters, from the territorial seas to the high seas (or international waters) are supposed to remain open to "innocent passage." In other words, member nations agree not to interfere with passage through the sea except in cases where such passage threatens the peace or security of their nation.[5]

In cases where UNCLOS provisions are contested, the International Tribunal for the Law of the Sea (ITLOS) is empowered to hear cases between member countries. The first official case brought before ITLOS was a 1997 case involving an oil tanker from Saint Vincent and the Grenadines that was detained by authorities from the nation of Guinea after moving into Guinea's EEZ. The United Nations also has the power to convene special tribunals to arbitrate disagreements between signatory nations.

Over the years, there have been several prominent instances in which a member nation has refused to recognize the authority of UN tribunals. For instance, in a 2013 incident, a Greenpeace boat, known as the Arctic Sunrise, engaged in protests against Russian oil drilling operations in the Pechora Sea. The Russian Coast Guard seized the ship and reported their intention to charge the passengers and crew as maritime "pirates." This resulted in the Netherlands asking for arbitration through ITLOS, with Russia refusing to acknowledge or participate in the tribunal. Though the activists were later released, Russia has since refused to recognize the court's determination, and the court of arbitration ruled in 2015 that Russia owes damages to the Netherlands over the seizure of the ship.[6]

China versus the Philippines

In 1951, Japan was forced to renounce its territorial claims to the Spratly Islands, which Japanese forces captured during World War II. However, after agreeing to renounce their claim, ownership of the Spratly Islands was undetermined. China released a statement asserting ownership over the archipelagos in the South China Sea, including the Spratly Islands. While China issued this claim, the nation did not, for many years, attempt to make any changes that affected other nations utilizing all or portions of the Spratly Island chain. Conflicts began to occur when China increased its presence in the region in the 2000s.[7] The Spratly Islands sit within a large swath of the South China sea claimed, in part or in whole, by China, and delineated by the "nine-dash" line and further claim that the nation's sovereign ownership of the islands is the basis for an expansion of their rightful territorial sea under UNCLOS.

Since the 1950s, China and the Philippines have repeatedly clashed over ownership of the Spratly Islands, Scarborough Shoal, and Mischief Reef, three of the most notable features within the South China Sea. The modern phase of this debate began in 2009, when China officially stated its claim to the Spratly Islands in a notice delivered to the United Nations. In 2013, the Philippines formally requested arbitration through UNCLOS, resulting in the establishment of a tribunal empowered to hear arguments in the case. China, however, refused to participate in establishing the tribunal, to appear before the tribunal, or to be bound by the results of any resulting arbitration. Among the fifteen separate accusations levied against China, the Philippines held that China's nine-dash line was illegitimate. China argued that the UN did not have the power to determine whether their nine-dash line system was valid, as the issue involved a determination of territorial sovereignty, which is beyond the scope of UNCLOS authority.

Features designated as islands, under UNCLOS, are given a 200-nautical mile zone surrounding the island, controlled by the nation claiming sovereignty. By contrast, an oceanic "rock," defined as a small terrestrial feature not substantial enough to warrant classification as an Island, is provided with a 12-nautical mile territorial zone. Another major feature of the case involved the fact that China's territorial claims passed within the Philippine EEZ and therefore whether China could legitimately claim sovereignty over territory within another nations EEZ.[8]

On July 12, 2016, the Permanent Court of Arbitration ruled that the establishment of UNCLOS, and China's agreement to abide by the convention, superseded any territorial claims that might be used to justify the nine-dash line. Further, the tribunal found that none of the Spratly Islands could be claimed to extend the continental shelf of China and so that the waters extending 200 miles from the coast of the Spratly Islands were either international waters or fell within the EEZ of one of the other neighboring countries. In addition, the court ruled that China had violated the Philippines EEZ and had unlawfully interfered with Philippine efforts to utilize resources within their territory. The ruling also struck at the heart of China's claims, stating that although there was evidence that Chinese fishermen and other sailors had long utilized the islands in the South China Sea, there was no evidence to suggest that China had ever exerted control over the region or that their historical use was in any way more significant than the historical use of the region by fishermen from the Philippines, Vietnam, or Malaysia.

China immediately released statements criticizing the tribunal's ruling and refusing to abide by the court's decision, alleging again that the issue was one of sovereignty and territorial boundaries, and therefore outside the jurisdiction of the tribunal. While the ruling resulted in celebrations in the Philippines, there was little international consensus on how to deal with the court's ruling, given that China refused to acknowledge the arbitration, demonstrating one of the profound difficulties with international law in the lack of effective means for enforcement. Over the subsequent year, amidst strong rhetoric between the United States and China, Chinese leaders engaged in bilateral meetings with the Philippines and other nations contesting their territorial claims, which muted, but did not eliminate, opposition to their activities among other Asian nations. Moving into 2018, it appeared unlikely that the UN ruling would affect China's policies and this raises important questions moving forward, such as how to more effectively enforce and strengthen UN law so as to make it possible to hold powerful nations responsive to international agreements.

Micah L. Issitt

Works Used

"Arbitration between the Republic of the Philippines and the People's Republic of China." *PCA*. Permanent Court of Arbitration. Oct 29 2015. Web. 16 Dec 2017.

"Factbox: What Trump Has Said about the United Nations." *Reuters*. Reuters. Sep 17 2017. Web. 16 Nov 2017.

"History of the United Nations." *UN*. United Nations. 2016. Web. 16 Nov 2017.

Kontorovich, Eugene. "Arctic Sunrise (Netherlands v. Russia)." *The American Journal of International Law*. Vol. 110, No. 1 (January 2016), 96-102.

"A Short History of The Hague." *Denhaag*. The Hague. 2016. Web. 15 Nov 2017.

"UN Documentation: International Law." *UN*. United Nations Dag Hammarskjöld Library. Nov 2017. Web. 18 Dec 2017.

"United Nations Convention on the Law of the Sea." *UN*. United Nations. May 4 2017. Web. 16 Nov 2017.

"Why Is the South China Sea Contentious?" *BBC*. BBC News. Jul 12 2016. Web. 16 Nov 2017.

Notes

1. "History of the United Nations," *UN*.
2. "Factbox: What Trump Has Said about the United Nations," *Reuters*.
3. "A Short History of the Hague," *Denhaag*.
4. "UN Documentation: International Law," *UN*.
5. "United Nations Convention on the Law of the Sea," *UN*.
6. Kontorovich, "Artic Sunrise (Netherlands v. Russia)."
7. "Why Is the South China Sea Contentious?" *BBC*.
8. "Arbitration between the Republic of the Philippines and the People's Republic of China," *PCA*.

The South China Sea: Explaining the Dispute

By Max Fisher, translator
The New York Times, July 14, 2016

WASHINGTON—After an international tribunal in The Hague ruled emphatically against China in a territorial dispute with the Philippines, many Chinese state media outlets responded on Wednesday by publishing a map. It showed the South China Sea, with most of the waters encircled with the "nine-dash line" that has long represented China's claims there.

This week's ruling may have delivered a sweeping victory in court to the Philippines, which argued that its maritime territory was being illegally seized by China. But it has only escalated the larger dispute, which involves several Asian nations as well as the United States, and which is as much about China's rise into a major world power as it is about this one sea.

What follows is an explanation of why this body of water is considered such a big deal, and why it may be a harbinger of global power politics in the decades ahead.

1. What Is the Dispute About?

At its most basic level, this is a contest between China and several Southeast Asian nations over territorial control in the South China Sea, which includes some of the most strategically important maritime territory on earth.

China, for the past few years, has been asserting ever greater control over faraway waters that were previously considered international or were claimed by other countries. For example, it has seized small land formations or reefs, sometimes dredging up underwater sediment to make the islands large enough to support small military installations.

China's naval forces have also grown more aggressive in patrolling these claims and chasing off non-Chinese ships. That is part of why its neighbors see this as an effort by China to dominate the region.

This is also about whether China will comply with international laws and norms, which Beijing sometimes views as a plot to constrain the country's rise.

The United States has gotten involved, sending the Navy to patrol waters it insists are international and backing international mediation efforts. Washington says it wants to maintain free movement and rule by international law. The risk of outright conflict is extremely low, but the militarization of these heavily trafficked and heavily fished waters is still dangerous.

2. What Does This Week's Ruling Mean?

The tribunal ruled almost categorically in favor of the Philippines, which had challenged some of China's territorial claims. It also said China had broken international law by endangering Philippine ships and damaging the marine environment.

Maybe most important, the tribunal largely rejected the nine-dash line that China has used to indicate its South China Sea claims. This could open the way for other Asian states to challenge China's claims.

So the letter of international law seems to say that China could be compelled to abandon many of its South China Sea claims.

But while the ruling is considered binding, there is no enforcement mechanism. China boycotted the proceedings, saying that the tribunal had no jurisdiction and that it would ignore any decision—a position it reiterated after the ruling came out.

> **The tribunal largely rejected the nine-dash line that China has used to indicate its South China Sea claims.**

Still, China is facing international pressure. Whether China chooses to defy or comply with that pressure, though, could help to shape its place in the international community.

3. What Is the "Nine-Dash Line"?

This little line has shown up on official Chinese maps since the 1940s (it began with 11 dashes). It demarcates a vast but vague stretch of ocean from China's southern coast through most of the South China Sea.

China has never clarified the line's exact coordinates. But it sweeps across waters—and some small islands—that are claimed by five other nations. It seems to go many miles beyond what is allowed under the United Nations treaty on maritime territorial issues, which China signed.

These are the areas where China has been building islands, installing runways and running patrols.

For China, the line represents long-lost historical claims that the country, after two centuries of weakness, is finally strong enough to recover. For the other nations, the line is a symbol of what they characterize as a naked power grab by China.

4. Why Is the South China Sea So Important?

The United States Energy Information Agency estimates there are 11 billion barrels of oil and 190 trillion cubic feet of natural gas in deposits under the sea—more than exists in the reserves of some of the world's biggest energy exporters.

The waters also contain lucrative fisheries that account for, according to some estimates, 10 percent of the global total. But this means that a lot of fishing boats are cruising around in waters contested by several different navies, increasing the risk of conflict.

The area's greatest value is as a trade route. According to a 2015 Department of Defense report, $5.3 trillion worth of goods moves through the sea every year, which is about 30 percent of global maritime trade. That includes huge amounts of oil and $1.2 trillion worth of annual trade with the United States.

5. Why Does It Matter Who Controls Those Trade Routes?

This gets to a core contradiction in the South China Sea dispute: It is driven by territorial competition, yet all countries involved want open sea routes. Everyone benefits from the free flow of goods between Asia and the rest of the world, and everyone suffers if that is disrupted.

This is part of why the United States stresses freedom of movement in international waters. While it is very unlikely that China would ever want to close off trade, the United States would still rather not allow Beijing even the ability to hold the global economy hostage.

But, from China's perspective, the United States itself has that ability, because of American naval dominance; the Chinese also suspect that the global status quo is engineered to serve Western interests first. So it is hardly surprising that China is seeking greater control over waterways it relies on for economic survival.

This is a dynamic that has permeated Sino-American relations throughout China's rise over the past two decades. In theory, both nations understand they are better off cooperating. But in practice, they often treat each other as competitors or potential threats—a cycle that is difficult to break.

6. So This Is about China's Rise?

In some ways, yes.

China sees itself as a growing power that has a right to further its interests in its own backyard, just as Western powers have done for centuries. Beijing considers the South China Sea an area of traditional Chinese influence, and sees its control as a way to assert greater power over the region.

Something Americans often miss is that for China, this is in part defensive. The history of Western imperialism looms large. Chinese leaders often distrust the United States' intentions, and consider their country to be the far weaker party. Extending Chinese control is a way to stave off perceived threats.

This insecurity also contributes to Chinese skepticism of international institutions such as the South China Sea tribunal, which Chinese state media portray as a plot to weaken China.

7. Why Is the United States So Involved in This?

The United States has a treaty obligation to the Philippines, an ally. As the world's largest economy, it also has a real interest in maintaining open sea lanes—and, as the world's biggest naval power, it often assumes the role of policing them. Plus, as the world's only superpower, the United States often acts as a balancer in regional disputes.

But this is also, for Washington, about shaping what sort of major power China becomes.

American officials insist that they do not oppose China's rise. Their concern is whether China will work within what scholars call the liberal order—the postwar system of international laws and institutions—or seek to overturn it.

The South China Sea, and particularly this week's ruling, are a test case for whether China becomes the kind of power that works within that system, or against it.

While that order has helped promote peace and prosperity globally, it also undeniably serves American interests.

Everyone agrees that the status quo in Asia and eventually the world will evolve to accommodate China's emergence as a major international power. The South China Sea is very important in its own right, but it is maybe most important in helping to determine what sort of role China plays in the world.

Print Citations

CMS: Fisher, Max, trans. "The South China Sea: Explaining the Dispute." In *The Reference Shelf: The South China Sea Conflict*, edited by Betsy Maury, 37-40. Ipswich, MA: H.W. Wilson, 2018.

MLA: Fisher, Max, trans. "The South China Sea: Explaining the Dispute." *The Reference Shelf: The South China Sea Conflict*. Ed. Betsy Maury. Ipswich: H.W. Wilson, 2018. 37-40. Print.

APA: Fisher, M., trans. (2018). The South China Sea: Explaining the dispute. In Betsy Maury (Ed.), *The reference shelf: The South China Sea conflict* (pp. 37-40). Ipswich, MA: H.W. Wilson. (Original work published 2016)

Progress in the South China Sea? A Year after the Hague Ruling

By Lynn Kuok
Foreign Affairs, July 21, 2017

July 12 marked the one-year anniversary of a United Nations tribunal ruling in a case brought by the Philippines against China over the latter's claims and activities in the South China Sea. The ruling was a major victory for the Philippines, particularly the tribunal's decision on China's "nine-dash line," through which Beijing attempts to lay claim to vast areas of the South China Sea. A year to the day after the award, the Philippines issued a conciliatory statement even as an energy official announced that Manila would soon offer investors new oil and gas blocks at Reed Bank, off the Philippine coast but within the nine-dash line.

Beijing, for its part, has always made clear that it regards the tribunal's decision as "null and void" and of "no binding force." Statements from Association of Southeast Asian Nations (ASEAN) states in the wake of the decision were muted. None urged China to adhere to the ruling; the strongest merely called for respecting international law.

Yet the impact of the decision cannot be determined by words alone. A year after the landmark award, ASEAN states appear to be more willing to assert their rights to resources in their exclusive economic zones (EEZs), and China's behavior is now more in keeping with the tribunal's decision.

Much Ado about Nothing?

Some media reports and analysts have dismissed the decision as entirely ineffective. Territorial disputes in the South China Sea continue to fester and are likely to do so for a long time. China's island-building, construction of facilities, and militarization of features in the area proceed unabated. The disagreement between China and the United States concerning rights concerning navigation, overflight, and military activities, manifested in U.S. freedom of navigation operations and China's objections to them, likewise persists.

But the tribunal was never meant to resolve those issues. It did not rule on who has a better claim to sovereignty over land features in the South China Sea—it had no jurisdiction to do so. Rather, it ruled on the status and maritime entitlements of features in the Spratlys, in the south, and Scarborough Shoal, off the Philippine island of Luzon. The case centered on the interpretation and application of the United Nations Convention on the Law of the Sea, which governs whether a feature is a full island entitled to a 200-nautical-mile EEZ, a rock entitled to only a 12-nautical-mile territorial sea, or a low-tide elevation or submerged feature not capable of independent sovereignty claims or generating any maritime zones of its own.

In addition, the tribunal did not rule on the lawfulness of China's island-building, facility construction, or militarization of high-tide features. It did, however, find that China's occupation of and construction on Mischief Reef, a low-tide elevation in the Philippines' EEZ and continental shelf, were problematic given that the feature falls within the Philippines' jurisdiction.

Finally, the decision has only indirect implications for U.S. freedom of navigation operations inasmuch as it clarified the status and maritime entitlements of features in the Spratlys. In turn, the Trump administration's first such operation asserted high-sea freedoms around Mischief Reef, a feature the tribunal found generates no territorial sea. Beijing's response was to (wrongly) claim that the exercise "infringed upon China's sovereignty" and to object that the maneuver was done without China's approval. Beijing insists on authorization before foreign warships can exercise the right of innocent passage in its territorial sea—a requirement not found in the UN Convention on the Law of the Sea. Beijing also dispatched military vessels and fighter planes to warn off the U.S. vessel.

Game Changer on Resource Rights

The real significance of the tribunal's decision was to clarify resource rights. Its main findings were twofold. First, it ruled that China cannot claim historic rights to resources in the waters within the nine-dash line if those waters are within the EEZs of other coastal states. Such rights were extinguished when China ratified the UN Convention on the Law of the Sea in 1996. Second, the tribunal ruled that none of the features in the Spratlys is entitled to a 200-nautical-mile EEZ. Like Scarborough Shoal, all of the Spratly features are at most rocks entitled to 12-nautical-mile territorial seas.

Although technically binding only on parties to the arbitration, the tribunal's decision has bolstered the position of ASEAN littoral states in the South China Sea. It has clarified that the EEZ entitlements of the Philippines, as well as Brunei, Indonesia, Malaysia, and Vietnam, are unencumbered by China's nine-dash line or any claimed EEZ from features in the Spratlys. Areas of overlap in the Spratlys are now limited to a 12-nautical-mile ring around rock features. Beyond these areas, China has no claim recognized under international law to fish or to extract oil or gas in the EEZs of other states outside the EEZ generated from China's mainland.

Beijing's Behavior

In assessing the impact of the award, what China and ASEAN states do is at least as important as what they say.

In official statements issued on the day of and after the judgment, Beijing appeared to expressly assert, for the first time, that China's maritime claims in the South China Sea include "historic rights." It did not specify what it means by this. However, if Beijing is claiming historic rights to resources within the entirety of the nine-dash line (rather than historic fishing rights within territorial seas), its assertion flies in the face of the judgment.

> **Southeast Asian states appear to be more willing to assert their rights to resources in their EEZs.**

In May this year, Beijing also imposed an annual fishing ban, which overlapped with the EEZs of the Philippines and Vietnam but excluded the Spratlys. The ban, which will be in place until September, is clearly problematic in light of the ruling.

However, the extent to which Beijing has actually sought to enforce the ban for non-Chinese fishing vessels in areas outside China's EEZ is unclear. There were reports in June of its targeting Vietnamese fishermen near the Paracels in the northern part of the South China Sea. But China, Taiwan, and Vietnam all claim sovereignty over these features, and their status and maritime entitlements were not considered by the tribunal.

In a positive sign, there have been no public reports of Chinese navy or coast guard vessels supporting illegal fishing within the Indonesian EEZ since the award. This is in stark contrast to highly publicized episodes in Indonesia's EEZ in March, May, and June 2016. In the first of these incidents, a Chinese coast guard vessel rammed an Indonesian law enforcement vessel to secure the release of a Chinese boat being towed away for illegal fishing.

Further, since October 2016, Beijing has also reportedly permitted Philippine and Vietnamese fishermen to return to Scarborough Shoal after blockading it since 2012. This move is consistent with the tribunal's ruling that fishermen from China, the Philippines, Taiwan, and Vietnam all enjoy traditional fishing rights in the territorial sea of Scarborough Shoal, and these rights were not extinguished by the UN Convention on the Law of the Sea.

A senior Chinese general reportedly cut short an official visit to Vietnam in June this year because of news that Hanoi had begun drilling in a disputed area that Beijing had previously leased out to a different entity. But Beijing has done nothing to stop Hanoi's drilling, nor has it made any public statement condemning it. The tribunal's award has made clear that China has no legitimate claim to resources in this area.

Beijing's response was far less bellicose than the threats of war it allegedly made in May this year after news that Manila wanted to develop Reed Bank. Exploration in this disputed area had been suspended in late 2014 while legal proceedings were ongoing. Beijing has not responded to Manila's latest announcement that it will resume drilling for oil and gas in December. How Beijing chooses to react in the event that Manila proceeds will be critical.

It is still too early to conclude that the tribunal's decision has positively shaped conduct in the South China Sea. But a careful examination of events since July 2016 suggests that ASEAN states appear to be more willing to assert their rights to resources in their EEZs and that Beijing (with the exception of its continued presence on and fortification of Mischief Reef) has kept its actions if not its words broadly within the letter of the ruling.

Whether Beijing's behavior should be attributed to its appreciation that flouting the ruling undermines trust and respect for China or to a more short-sighted desire to avoid direct confrontation just before its critical nineteenth party congress in September remains an open question. Whatever the case, respect for international law is critical to China's long-term interests in peace and stability. Beijing will do well to recognize this and act accordingly.

Print Citations

CMS: Kuok, Lynn. "Progress in the South China Sea? A Year after the Hague Ruling." In *The Reference Shelf: The South China Sea Conflict*, edited by Betsy Maury, 41-44. Ipswich, MA: H.W. Wilson, 2018.

MLA: Kuok, Lynn. "Progress in the South China Sea? A Year after the Hague Ruling." *The Reference Shelf: The South China Sea Conflict*. Ed. Betsy Maury. Ipswich: H.W. Wilson, 2018. 41-44. Print.

APA: Kuok, L. (2018). Progress in the South China Sea? A year after the Hague ruling. In Betsy Maury (Ed.), *The reference shelf: The South China Sea conflict* (pp. 41-44). Ipswich, MA: H.W. Wilson. (Original work published 2017)

Explainer: What Are the Legal Implications of the South China Sea Ruling?

By Clive Schofield
The Conversation, July 13, 2016

The ruling in the case brought by the Philippines against China's activities in the South China Sea is significant—not just because it involves China, but because it tackles key ambiguities and uncertainties in the United Nations Convention on the Law of the Sea (UNCLOS).

The Decision

Both China and the Philippines are parties to UNCLOS. As it arose from the convention, the tribunal that heard the case could not resolve the core sovereignty issues at stake—that is, who owns which feature.

The key findings can be summarised as follows:

- Any historic rights to resources in the waters within China's apparent claim to areas within the so-called nine-dash line were extinguished where they were incompatible with the maritime zones set out under UNCLOS.

- None of the disputed above-high-tide features in the Spratly Islands, individually or collectively, are capable of generating extended maritime claims (beyond a 12-nautical-mile territorial sea).

- China has violated the sovereign rights of the Philippines in its exclusive economic zone (EEZ) by interfering with Philippine fishing and petroleum exploration activities, constructing artificial islands, and failing to prevent Chinese fishermen from fishing in the Philippines' EEZ.

- China has caused severe harm to the coral reef environment and violated its obligation to preserve and protect fragile ecosystems and the habitat of depleted, threatened or endangered species through its recent large-scale land reclamation and construction of artificial islands on seven features in the South China Sea.

- China has aggravated the dispute since the start of the arbitration process, particularly through large-scale land reclamation and artificial island construction activities, which have inflicted irreparable harm on the marine environment.

Reinforcing the Rule of Law at Sea

By tackling key "unfinished business" in the Law of the Sea, especially countering apparently historically inspired unilateral claims to maritime spaces, as well as clarifying the status of insular features and their capacity to generate broad maritime claims, the decision is hugely significant for the Law of the Sea's development and international law generally.

UNCLOS is a remarkable treaty. Almost all countries subscribe to it. While it is notable that the United States is not a party, the US nonetheless conducts its maritime claims and policies in line with the convention's terms.

A key achievement of the convention was agreement on an overarching spatial framework of maritime claims. This includes a territorial sea out to 12 nautical miles and an EEZ out to a 200-nautical-mile limit. These expansions of maritime claims offshore are balanced by the rights of other states in these zones—for example, by guaranteeing freedom of navigation.

Exceptions to the rule threaten this structure. Some countries sign up to the convention's terms but still try to maintain more expansive unilateral claims, often justified on hazy historical grounds.

This ruling arguably closes loopholes and counters temptations to engage in exceptionalism on the part of some countries.

Does It Matter?

The decision undoubtedly represents a sweeping victory for the Philippines. It is, however, unenforceable. And from the outset China has refused to recognise the tribunal's jurisdiction.

China's reaction to the verdict was swift and uncompromising. A Foreign Ministry statement declared the decision was "null and void with no binding force".

Nonetheless, the tribunal did evaluate whether it had the jurisdiction to hear the case. For the most part, it determined it did on questions related to the Law of the Sea. As far as the tribunal is concerned, the award is legally binding on China as a party to UNCLOS.

China appears highly likely to simply ignore the ruling, at least in the near term. Its vigorous opposition to the decision may also lead to escalation—for instance, an intensification of China's island-building campaign in new locations and an increase in enforcement actions within the nine-dash line. This may lead to a proliferation of incidents with other South China Sea countries and a distinct rise in regional tensions.

The decision's longer-term value may be profound, however. It fundamentally undermines key aspects of China's position in the South China Sea. This will undoubtedly inform future interactions between China and its neighbours.

> **The guardedly good news is China has already indicated it will seek to "maintain peace and stability in the South China Sea" in accordance with international law.**

The guardedly good news is China has already indicated it will seek to "maintain peace and stability in the South China Sea" in accordance with international law.

This indicates it is unlikely to disrupt freedom of navigation and trade through a water body that carries US$5 trillion per year in trade. That includes almost one-third of the global oil trade, over half of global liquefied natural gas exports and more than half of Australia's international trade by value.

Implications beyond the South China Sea

The ruling has the potential to reach far beyond the South China Sea and transform the international maritime map.

It indicates historic claims cannot be readily sustained. This undermines the unilateral claims of certain countries—such as Canada's historical claims related to its Arctic archipelago.

Even though the ruling is technically only binding on China and the Philippines, it carries considerable legal weight as an authoritative and unanimous ruling by an international judicial body. As a result of uncertainties over which insular features can generate what maritime zones, many countries have advanced expansive maritime claims from small islands. These claims are now in jeopardy.

For example, the US claims 200-nautical-mile EEZs from several remote Pacific island territories that appear remarkably similar to some of the South China Sea features that the tribunal found could not generate extended maritime claims. The US welcomed the ruling, but it will be intriguing to see whether the US and other countries modify their practices in light of it.

Print Citations

CMS: Schofield, Clive. "Explainer: What Are the Legal Implications of the South China Sea Ruling?" In *The Reference Shelf: The South China Sea Conflict*, edited by Betsy Maury, 45-47. Ipswich, MA: H.W. Wilson, 2018.

MLA: Schofield, Clive. "Explainer: What Are the Legal Implications of the South China Sea Ruling?" *The Reference Shelf: The South China Sea Conflict*. Ed. Betsy Maury. Ipswich: H.W. Wilson, 2018. 45-47. Print.

APA: Schofield, C. (2018). Explainer: What are the legal implications of the South China Sea ruling? In Betsy Maury (Ed.), *The reference shelf: The South China Sea conflict* (pp. 45-47). Ipswich, MA: H.W. Wilson. (Original work published 2016)

Here's Why the South China Sea Dispute Will Continue to Haunt Philippine-China Relations

By Richard Javan Heydarian
Huffington Post, July 25, 2017

MANILA, Philippines—A year has passed since the South China Sea arbitration case at The Hague, and many are still wondering whether the Philippines has benefited from the landmark award at all. Despite Philippine President Rodrigo Duterte's best efforts to downplay territorial disputes with China in favor of stronger strategic and economic ties, the South China Sea continues to haunt bilateral relations between the two neighbors.

Beyond Manila's wildest dreams, the arbitral tribunal, which was constituted under Article 287, Annex VII of the United Nations Convention on the Law of the Sea, or UNCLOS, ruled heavily against China. It nullified China's doctrine of "historic rights," which has served as the foundation of Beijing's expansive nine-dash line claims across much of the South China Sea basin.

According to the tribunal, China's claims, based on pre-modern maps and historical events, are "incompatible" with prevailing international law, especially since "there was no evidence that China had historically exercised exclusive control over the waters or their resources" in the South China Sea. The decision went a step further, censuring China for "violat[ing] the Philippines' sovereign rights," specifically by coercively preventing the Southeast Asian country from exploiting hydrocarbon deposits and fisheries stock within its own exclusive economic zone, or EEZ.

Contrary to China's claims, the tribunal also ruled that there were no naturally formed "islands" in the Spratly chain, thus none of the contested land features can generate their own EEZs. The tribunal also ruled against China's massive reclamation activities in the area, describing them as "incompatible with the obligations" of member states, especially because they "inflicted irreparable harm to the maritime environment" as well as "destroyed evidence of the natural condition of features" in the area.

In legal terms, the verdict is final and binding, per Article 296 as well as Article 11 of Annex VII of the convention. Predictably, China first adopted the "three no's" attitude of non-recognition, non-participation and non-compliance towards the

---

decision, which it dismissed as "null and void" and "nothing more than a piece of paper."

As months went by, China tried to bury the issue altogether as if the arbitration proceedings never happened, while proposing to set up its own international arbitration bodies as an alternative to the supposedly Western-dominated courts under the existing global order. Beijing also proceeded with a systematic campaign to denigrate, distort and delegitimize not only the arbitral tribunal, but also its panel of judges. It even threatened to withdraw from UNCLOS altogether, while managing to convince, cajole and pressure many countries, including several members of the Association of Southeast Asian Nations, or ASEAN, to downplay, dismiss or ignore the award.

The Obama administration, which strongly supported the Philippines' legal warfare strategy, also took a soft position. It called for calm and patience while deploying then-National Security Adviser Susan Rice to Beijing to ease China's nerves. With the exception of Japan and Australia, which categorically called for complaisance by both parties, few countries fully stood by the Philippines' side.

Yet China's ace in the hole was none other than Rodrigo Duterte, the newly inaugurated president of the Philippines, who immediately took a different line on the disputes. Instead of celebrating the country's undisputed victory against China, Duterte made it clear that he wasn't interested in flaunting the verdict, and wanted to focus on a soft landing in the South China Sea.

Then-Philippine Foreign Secretary Perfecto Yasay Jr. immediately called for "restraint and sobriety." In succeeding months, Duterte dispatched former Philippine President Fidel V. Ramos to restore bilateral diplomatic ties with China. This paved the way for Duterte's state visit to Beijing last October, in which he declared his preference for strategic "separation" from the United States in favor of new alliances with China and Russia.

Duterte's soft-pedaling has provoked heavy criticism from several quarters at home.

As a gesture of goodwill, Duterte refused to raise the arbitration award in regional fora, including in ASEAN, which he currently chairs. He even blocked any criticism of China's massive reclamation activities and establishment of military facilities in the Spratly chain of islands, where the Philippines controls up to nine land features, including Thitu Island.

Duterte also canceled various joint military exercises with the United States in the South China Sea, while nixing initial plans for joint patrols in the area. In exchange, China has offered a multi-billion dollar package of infrastructure investment and a $500 million loan to the Philippines' military.

Since then, the two countries have rapidly normalized their bilateral relations, upgraded investment ties, and are currently contemplating tightening defense relations. Pleased with the direction of bilateral relations, Chinese Foreign Minister Wang Yi described bilateral relations with the Philippines as entering a "golden period of fast development."

As Manila marked the first anniversary of the arbitration award, newly-installed Foreign Affairs Secretary Alan Peter Cayetano maintained that "the ongoing territorial dispute in the [South China Sea] should further be resolved in a manner consistent with the spirit of good neighborly relations." Philippine ambassador to China Jose Santiago "Chito" Santa Romana emphasized the importance of "pragmatism" given the necessity to bridge differences, rather than just focusing on principle alone.

Yet, Duterte's soft-pedaling has provoked heavy criticism from several quarters at home. Philippine Supreme Court Justice Antonio Carpio, who played an advisory role in the arbitration award, described the government's approach as lacking "discernible direction, coherence or vision."

And Duterte's controversial remarks, particularly the late 2016 announcement that he "will set aside the arbitral ruling," have been a source of concern among those who view Philippine foreign policy as too acquiescent towards China.

"This incident [Duterte's remark] graphically explains Philippine foreign policy on the South China Sea dispute after the arbitral ruling," Carpio lamented during a high-profile symposium marking the first anniversary of the arbitration award.

"The Duterte administration refused to celebrate the ruling, even though the ruling legally secured for the Philippines a vast maritime zone larger than the total land area of the Philippines," he continued. The influential magistrate has enjoined the government to consider, among other things, filing additional arbitration cases against China if the latter continues to ignore the ruling.

Other influential members of the defense establishment, including former Philippine Foreign Affairs Secretary Albert del Rosario, have echoed his criticisms in recent months, much to the chagrin of the president. Even some experts, such as Jay Batongbacal, the country's leading maritime law expert, have accused the government of softening its position in exchange for Chinese investments.

So far, the Philippines has only managed to secure a provisional and limited modus vivendi with China in the South China Sea. Filipino fishermen have been allowed to operate in the immediate vicinity of the hotly contested Scarborough Shoal, which is currently under the administrative control of Chinese coast guard vessels.

But they haven't been allowed to enter the lagoon within the shoal, which is rich in fisheries stock and serves as a crucial rest, repair and recuperation spot for fishermen, especially during stormy seasons. Many experts are also skeptical whether the recently agreed upon outline of a framework for a code of conduct in the South China Sea will have any consequential impact on China's activities in the area.

In the meantime, China continues to expand its military footprint across disputed land features, provoking anxieties among the Philippines defense-intelligentsia-media establishment. There are worries about the possibility of China building structures on the Scarborough Shoal as well as expanding its areas of claim into the Philippines' eastern shores, particularly Benham Rise.

What happens next remains to be seen, but it is clear that in the coming months and years, Duterte is bound to face growing pressure to raise the arbitration award in bilateral and multilateral fora.

Print Citations

CMS: Heydarian, Richard Javan. "Here's Why the South China Sea Dispute Will Continue to Haunt Philippine-China Relations." In *The Reference Shelf: The South China Sea Conflict*, edited by Betsy Maury, 48-51. Ipswich, MA: H.W. Wilson, 2018.

MLA: Heydarian, Richard Javan. "Here's Why the South China Sea Dispute Will Continue to Haunt Philippine-China Relations." *The Reference Shelf: The South China Sea Conflict*. Ed. Betsy Maury. Ipswich: H.W. Wilson, 2018. 48-51. Print.

APA: Heydarian, R.J. (2018). Here's why the South China Sea dispute will continue to haunt Philippine-China relations. In Betsy Maury (Ed.), *The reference shelf: The South China Sea conflict* (pp. 48-51). Ipswich, MA: H.W. Wilson. (Original work published 2017)

3
Competing Claims

Protesters holding placards and streamers shout anti-China slogans during a protest against China's presence in disputed waters in the South China Sea, in front of the Chinese consulate in the financial district of Manila on June 12, 2017, to coincide with the Philippines' Independence Day celebrations.

Competing Claims: International Interests in the South China Sea

Depending on perspective, the South China Sea conflict can be seen as an economic issue, a matter of sovereignty, a factor in the ongoing effort to preserve oceanic resources, or a test of the stability and rigor of United Nations and international law. The nations involved in the conflict each have unique claims to portions of the sea as well as political, social, and economic reasons for taking part in the debate. Examining each nation's interests and the steps they've taken in the controversy, demonstrates the complexity of international politics and helps elucidate the importance of the issue for both the major players, and the world.

China

China's claims to the South China Sea are not based on proximity, but rather to a complex sovereignty claim based on the contention that Chinese explorers and settlers established ancient communities in the sea. China's Ministry of Foreign Affairs claims that China was the first nation to discover and name the islands and references to the islands are found in books dating back as far as the Han Dynasty (216 BCE–220 CE). Claims over the Paracel and Spratly Islands are thus, in part, derived from ancient maps and other historic texts indicating a Chinese presence or at least commercial use of the seas surrounding the islands. China's ownership was the subject of a 2015-2016 arbitration in the Hague, with China rejecting the legitimacy of the trial, that resulted in the determination that China's historic and physical claims are largely invalid and superseded by the agreements that China made to the United Nations Convention on the Law of the Sea (UNCLOS).[1]

China has taken military possession of, and engaged in extensive dredging operations within, its claimed portion of the sea, towards the goal of transforming Subi Reef, Gaven Reefs, Fiery Cross Reef, Cuarteron Reef, Johnson South Reef, Mischief Reef, and Huges Reef into artificial islands. In 2017, it was revealed that China had effectively militarized a number of the occupied islands though the construction of artificial islands does not legally allow the nation to increase its territory under UNCLOS.[2]

Vietnam

Vietnam also claims historic rights to the Paracel and Spratly archipelagos based on long-term economic development of portions of the islands and international recognition of ownership. The government has presented documents indicating that Vietnamese fishing communities were utilizing the Paracels in the early seventeenth century, with a seventeenth century atlas describing the Paracel and Spratly Islands as being under the control of the Nguyen family of Vietnam. In addition, Portuguese and Dutch maps of the region from the seventeenth century identify the Paracels as part of Vietnamese territory. Bolstering this claim, Vietnamese scholars announced in 2016 the discovery of two historic maps detailing the extent of Chinese territory during the 1700s and 1800s, with neither map indicating that China controlled the Paracel or Spratly archipelagos at that time.[3]

Vietnam also claims that, during the period when Vietnam was occupied by the French, the French effectively claimed ownership and administration over the Paracels and Spratly islands, constituting a lawful establishment of sovereignty, and that, when France returned control of Vietnam to the Vietnamese, France legitimately transferred sovereignty to Vietnam in accordance with international law.

In a 2014 analysis by the CNA Corporation, a nonprofit specializing in naval policy, researchers determined that Vietnam had the stronger, more recent, and more comprehensive claim to both the Paracel and Spratly islands, compared to China. This results from the fact that Vietnam took a more systematic approach to establishing sovereignty in the eighteenth century, while the Chinese did not try to demonstrate sovereignty until 1909, and because China did not dispute France's claims to the Spratly and Paracel islands while France occupied Vietnam and therefore had no legal grounds to dispute France transferring sovereignty to Vietnam.[4]

The Philippines

The Philippines archipelago has asserted ownership over Scarborough Shoal, and a collection of 50 Spratly Island features, known collectively as the Kalayaan Island Group. Scarborough Shoal remains above water at high tide and is therefore a legitimate territory for claims of sovereignty, however, there is little historical evidence to bolster the Phillipine claim of ownership. In a 2014 analysis, the CNA Corporation found that neither China nor the Philippines had a strong physical or historic claim to Scarborough Shoal, though the Philippines was the first country to conduct an official survey of the feature. Further, the fact that the Shoal is 400 nautical miles closer to the Philippines than to China and sits within the Philippine exclusive economic zone (EEZ), strengthens the archipelago's claim over the shoal.

As for the parts of the Spratly Islands claimed by the Philippines, the CNA found that neither the Philippines nor China were able to present a sufficiently convincing historical claim of ownership, in comparison with Vietnam. However, the CNA found further that the Philippines has a superior claim to four high elevation features within the Spratly Islands: West York, Nanshan Island, Flat Island, and Lankiam Cay.[5]

Despite having strong claims only to Scarborough Shoal and a small portion of the Spratly Islands group, the Philippines had been, until 2017, the most outspoken opponent of Chinese development. The Philippines took their case to the United Nations in 2013, after a series of violent altercations with Chinese military. In 2016, the United Nations Permanent Court of Arbitration ruled that China's policies violate UNCLOS provisions, including the proposed nine-dash line, and asserted the Philippines right to Scarborough Shoal as part of the nation's EEZ. In response to the ruling, which China rejected, China threatened military action against the Philippines if the nation attempted to enforce the ruling. President Rodrigo Duterte, elected in 2016, quickly backed off the issue, in part responding to China's promise of economic support as long as the nation abandoned its maritime claims.[6]

Indonesia

Indonesia was a minor voice in the South China Sea debate until the 2016 UN tribunal ruling against China's nine-dash line. Indonesia used the court's ruling to reassert its legal right to territories falling within the nation's EEZ, though these claims were refuted by China. In July of 2017, Indonesia announced it was renaming its portion of the South China Sea, the North Natuna Sea, which surrounds the disputed, but Indonesian-controlled Natuna Islands.[7] The decision to provocatively rename their portion of the sea signaled a renewed interest on the part of the nation as well as a willingness to challenge China if backed by the United Nations. Though China criticized the renaming announcement and continued to assert ownership over the contested features, the territories controlled by Indonesia remain a minor concern for China and thus have not become a major part of the debate through 2018.

Malaysia and Brunei

In March of 2017, Malaysian foreign minister Anifah Aman released the strongest statement from Malaysia concerning the South China Sea debate, asserting ownership over the oceanic features falling within Malaysia's EEZ and rejecting the legitimacy of China's nine-dash line policy. Aman's unexpectedly bold statements were seemingly at odds with the standard governmental stance to that point, with Malaysian leaders having been reluctant to openly challenge China's position.[8]

According to an analysis by CNA, Malaysia claims ownership over a total of seven islands or rocks in the Spratly group, two of which are occupied by Vietnam and one by the Philippines. Malaysia has occupied the other four and has constructed mini-naval stations and boat docks on each of these features. The nation also claims ownership over three submerged reefs sitting on the nation's continental shelf. Malaysia claims ownership over Swallow Reef, which is an island and thus entitled to a 200-nautical mile EEZ, as well as the rocks of Erica Reef, Investigator Shaol, and Mariveles Reef, each of which generate a 12-nautical mile territorial sea. Malaysia also claims ownership of Amboyna Cay and Barque Canada Reef, both of which are occupied by Vietnam, and Commodore Reef/Rizal Reef, which is occupied by the Philippines.

The island nation of Brunei makes only a single claim to any portion of the contested Spratly Islands, Louisa Reef. The reef sits on Brunei's continental shelf, but it also claimed by Vietnam and China on the basis of historic sovereignty. The legitimacy of the claim also depends on whether Louisa Reef is determined to be an island or a low-tide elevation or submerged feature, in which case it would not be subject to occupation and would simply become part of Brunei's continental shelf.

If Louisa Reef is determined to be an island, the feature would then be subject to appropriation claims and would generate a territorial and exclusive use zone.[9]

Japan and the United States

Japan occupied several islands in the South China Sea during World War II, but was forced to surrender its territories in the wake of the war. In 2016 and 2017, Japan took a more aggressive interest in the South China Sea controversy, pledging support to the United States and to participate in US freedom of navigation and military exercises within the disputed area. Though the nation has no claims of sovereignty within the sea, Japan has strong commercial interests in maintaining access to the sea for shipping and views China as its strongest competitor within the region. China's territorial claims threaten Japan's trade agreements with several nations also claiming ownership over South China Sea waters. Under Prime Minister Shinzo Abe, Japan has also begun to take a more aggressive military policy overall. Abe's new direction for Japan's military, described by Abe as a "proactive peace diplomacy," may represent a fundamental change of power moving forward. Since World War II, and Japan's surrender, the nation has maintained a largely defensive military, and has engaged in few interventionist operations. Working with the United States, Japan began sending military vessels to the South China Sea to perform drills as well as promising to concentrate naval deployment to the sea by 2020, which is also a mirror of US policy.[10] While still a minor player in the South China Sea debate, Japan's 2016 and 2017 activities may suggest a stronger role for the island nation moving forward.[11]

Like Japan, the United States sees China as one of its strongest global rivals for power. The rivalry between the United States and China, as the world's two largest economies, has taken many different forms over the first 18 years of the twentieth-first century. Economists predict that the Chinese economy will overtake the United States as the world's largest economy before 2030 and the fear of this shift in power has influenced many aspects of US-China relations. In Lyle Goldstein's 2015 book, *Meeting China Halfway*, the author and political analyst argues that China/ US relations are plagued by fundamental distrust, creating an "escalation spiral" of increasing animosity. Goldstein proposes ten key areas, of which the South China Sea is one, where the United States has opportunities to work with China towards mutual goals, thus creating what Goldstein calls "cooperation spirals" that, gradually, bring the two nations closer and help to align global goals and opportunities.[12]

Unlike Vietnam, Indonesia, the Philippines, and Malaysia, the United States has no territorial claims in the South China sea and has only indirect security interests. Writing about the issue in *Foreign Policy* magazine, Robert Manning, of the Brent Scowcroft Center on International Security, argues that US core interests are not really at stake and that China knows that the United States will only go so far to intervene.[13] As of 2018, US policy in the sea has centered on conducting symbolic military operations to reassert freedom of navigation, but the United States has not yet managed to engage in any meaningful negotiation with China over the issue. As China has worked to solidify relations with other Asian nations, thus building support for their maritime program and eliminating direct competition, the role for the United States has become unclear and it remains to be seen whether the conflict will escalate or could become an arena for future cooperation.

Micah L. Issitt

Works Used

Allard, Tom and Munthe, Bernadette Christina. "Asserting Sovereignty, Indonesia Renamed Part of South China Sea." *Reuters*. Reuters Inc. Jul 14 2017. Web. 16 Dec 2017.

"China's Claims in the South China Sea." *The Wall Street Journal*. Dow Jones & Company. May 27 2015. Web. 16 Dec 2017.

"China's Maritime Disputes." *CFR*. Council on Foreign Relations. Jan 2017. Web. 16 Dec 2017.

Daiss, Tim. "Newly Found Maps Dispute Beijing's South China Sea Claims." *Forbes*. Forbes, Inc. Jun 1 2016. Web. 16 Dec 2017.

Drifte, Reinhard. "Japan's Policy towards the South China Sea—Applying 'Proactive Peace Diplomacy'?" *PRIF*. Peace Research Institute Frankfurt. 2016. Web. 16 Dec 2017.

Goldstein, Lyle J. *Meeting China Halfway: How to Defuse the Emerging US-China Rivalry*. Washington, DC: Georgetown University Press, 2015.

Hutt, David. "Malaysia Speaks Softly in the South China Sea." *Asia Times*. Asia Times Holding Limited. Mar 23 2017. Web. 16 Dec 2017.

Jozuka, Emiko. "Japan to Join US in South China Sea Patrols." *CNN*. CNN. Sep 16 2016. Web. 16 Dec 2017.

Manning, Robert A. and James Przystup. "Stop the South China Sea Charade." *Foreign Policy*. FP Group. Aug 17 2017. Web. 17 Dec 2017.

Mourdoukoutas, Panos. "In The South China Sea, Duterte's Playing China against America and Japan—Nicely." *Forbes*. Forbes, Inc. Nov 3 2017. Web. 16 Dec 2017.

Pedrozo, Raul. "China versus Vietnam: An Analysis of the Competing Claims in the South China Sea." *CNA Corporation*. CNA. Aug 2014. Web. 16 Dec 2017.

Roach, J. Ashley. "Malaysia and Brunei: An Analysis of Their Claims in the South China Sea." *CNA Corporation*. Aug 2014. Web. 16 Dec 2017.

Rosen, Mark E. "Philippine Claims in the South China Sea: A Legal Analysis." *CNA Corporation*. CNA. Aug 2014. Web. 16 Dec 2017.

Notes

1. "China's Maritime Disputes," *CFR*.
2. "China's Claims in the South China Sea," *The Wall Street Journal*.
3. Daiss, "Newly Found Maps Dispute Beijing's South China Sea Claims."
4. Pedrozo, "China versus Vietnam: An Analysis of the Competing Claims in the South China Sea."
5. Rosen, "Philippine Claims in the South China Sea: A Legal Analysis."

6. Mourdoukoutas, "In the South China Sea, Duterte's Playing China against America and Japan—Nicely."
7. Allard and Munthe, "Asserting Sovereignty, Indonesia Renames Part of South China Sea."
8. Hutt, "Malaysia Speaks Softly in the South China Sea."
9. Roach, "Malaysia and Brunei: An Analysis of Their Claims in the South China Sea."
10. Jozuka, "Japan to Join US in South China Sea Patrols."
11. Drifte, "Japan's Policy towards the South China Sea—Applying 'Proactive Peace Diplomacy'?"
12. Goldstein, *Meeting China Halfway: How to Defuse the Emerging US-China Rivalry.*
13. Manning and Przystup, "Stop the South China Sea Charade."

Vietnam Is Challenging China's Control of the Disputed South China Sea

By Ralph Jennings
Forbes, November 28, 2016

Leaders in Malaysia, Indonesia and the Philippines take a pragmatic, work-with-me-please view toward China in easing Asia's widest reaching sovereignty dispute. They all say the South China Sea, or some fragment of it, is theirs and their claims overlap. China has expanded quickly since 2010 to assert control over almost the entire 3.5 million-square-km (1.4 million-square-mile) sea, putting other countries on the defensive. But one other country is doing the same thing and China can neither ignore it nor neutralize it through economic and trade deals. (That's what happens to other countries.) It's almost China's double. It's Vietnam.

Vietnam is smaller than China and its military, ranked 17th by the database GlobalFirePower.com, lags China's at No. 3. But otherwise the two are chasing maritime control in the same ways. Here are five:

1. Both make historic claims. Beijing cites maps and documents going back to the Han Dynasty 2,200 years ago to substantiate its claim to the South China Sea. Vietnamese people were using the Spratly Islands, the sea's biggest group of tiny land features, as long as 1,000 years ago, their story goes. Hanoi has also cited an 1887 Franco-Chinese Treaty as a basis for allocating claims, though U.N. law questions the concept behind it, according to one scholar.

2. China and Vietnam assert more than the customary continental shelf. Vietnam's claim reaches past a conventional, internationally exclusive economic zone 200-nautical mile (370-km) from its Indochinese coastline into the Spratly archipelago, among other places. Its military units occupy the group's largest feature, Spratly Island. Claimants Brunei, Malaysia and the Philippines normally operate within 200 nautical miles of their shores. China claims nearly the whole resource-rich sea.

3. Both countries are reclaiming land for military use. China has landfilled about 3,200 acres (1,294 hectares) of land to beef up tiny, partly submerged islets. It's got surface-to-air missiles on Woody Island in the Paracel chain, to cite one example. Vietnam has landfilled 27 islets, more than any other claimant. It is investing now

> **China has expanded quickly since 2010 to assert control over almost the entire 3.5 million-square-km (1.4 million-square mile) sea, putting other countries on the defensive.**

in the extension of Spratly Island's runway from 2,500 to 3,300 feet, ideal for landing air force maritime surveillance aircraft, and building hangars, the U.S. think tank Center for Strategic and International Studies says. "Vietnam is the only other country there that has overlapping claims with China," says Carl Thayer, emeritus professor of politics at the University of New South Wales in Australia. "They both claim everything essentially. It's also the only other country to engage in such a robust defense modernization."

4. Nationalist crowds at home. The Communist governments of China and Vietnam must please home audiences with a keen sense of nationalism, including a deep historic resentment in Vietnam against the Chinese. The two sides talk of cooperation to avoid a nationalistic spillover such as the anti-China riots in Vietnam in 2014. But each uses is state-controlled mass media to remind an eager public of its claims. Local media cover Vietnamese island reclamation work to stoke excitement, for example, says Mekong Economics chief economist Adam McCarty.

5. Neither side is afraid of a fight. Scores died in 1974, and again in 1988, when Chinese and Vietnamese vessels clashed in the South China Sea. Most of the dead were Vietnamese sailors. In 2014, vessels from both sides rammed each other after Beijing let the Chinese offshore oil driller position a rig in the disputed Gulf of Tonkin. Now Vietnam is preparing for any new fights by accepting maritime patrol boats from Japan and military aid of $18 million from the United States.

Print Citations

CMS: Jennings, Ralph. "Vietnam Is Challenging China's Control of the Disputed South China Sea." In *The Reference Shelf: The South China Sea Conflict*, edited by Betsy Maury, 61-62. Ipswich, MA: H.W. Wilson, 2018.

MLA: Jennings, Ralph. "Vietnam Is Challenging China's Control of the Disputed South China Sea." *The Reference Shelf: The South China Sea Conflict*. Ed. Betsy Maury. Ipswich: H.W. Wilson, 2018. 61-62. Print.

APA: Jennings, R. (2018). "Vietnam is challenging China's control of the disputed South China Sea." In Betsy Maury (Ed.), *The reference shelf: The South China Sea conflict* (pp. 61-62). Ipswich, MA: H.W. Wilson. (Original work published 2016)

Why Is the South China Sea So Important to the US?

By Leszek Buszynski
The Conversation, January 18, 2017

Donald Trump's nominee for Secretary of State Rex Tillerson made some surprising remarks about China and the South China Sea during his recent Senate confirmation hearings. He said the US should "send China a clear signal that, first, the island-building stops, and second, your access to those islands also is not going to be allowed."

His comments created a furor in the international media as it seems the US might resort to force by blockading the Chinese-occupied features in the South China Sea.

James Mattis, Trump's defence secretary nominee, was more circumspect in his remarks to the Senate Armed Services Committee. He identified defence of so-called "international waters" as the "bottom line" for the US, suggesting the US would defend freedom of navigation in the South China Sea without challenging the Chinese presence there.

Mattis' comments were in line with US policy towards the South China Sea while Tillerson's remarks were not. But why is the South China Sea so important to the US anyway?

The Chinese regularly castigate the Americans for "meddling" in the area and have difficulty understanding why the US takes a stand on the issue. In their view, the US is making trouble for China and preventing its rise as a great power. The Chinese want to see the Americans abandon the South China Sea and withdraw from the western Pacific.

Some commentators in the US and elsewhere agree. They argue that this would allow America to forge an accommodation with China, which would remove the prospect of conflict between the world's two largest economies and bring peace and stability.

Others have called for a G-2 or a US-China accord that would settle global problems. They claim that the US is already overstretched and should return to the "offshore" position that it had before the Korean war broke out in 1950. Why let the South China Sea get in the way of this possible accommodation?

Chinese Regional Presence

The South China Sea has become important to the US because of China's challenge to the liberal rules-based order that America has promoted since the Pacific war. The post-war regional order was based on the American presence, which set the stage for impressive economic growth and regional prosperity without the threat of war or conflict.

It ensured that maritime disputes and territorial claims would be resolved through negotiation and not military power. And it served as the basis for the development of trade and regional economic relations from which all countries in the region benefited.

America's concern with the South China Sea is a result of China's effort to secure control over the maritime territory and the resources it contains. China insists on "indisputable sovereignty" over the area but a number of other claimants—Vietnam, Brunei, Malaysia and the Philippines—have the law on their side.

All have exclusive economic zones (EEZS) in the South China Sea, which is their right under UN Convention of the Law of the Sea (UNCLOS), and which the Chinese dismiss. To clarify the matter, the Philippines appealed to an tribunal convened under UNCLOS to rule on the situation.

In July 2016, the tribunal issued its judgement and upheld the rights of the ASEAN claimants to their EEZs, noting that the Chinese claim had no legal basis. China, however, has ignored legality in this dispute and is prepared to back its claim with military power. If it does not recognise the rules, the regional order that the US has been promoting breaks up.

China has militarised the Spratly Islands by engaging in reclamation projects in the South China Sea. The Chinese have been dredging sand from the ocean floor and extending the size of seven reefs they have occupied.

They have constructed three airfields there, two are 3,000 metres in length, one is 2,600 metres. These airfields can support military aircraft including bombers and large transport aircraft. With this military presence, China would be able to control the South China Sea. And its strengthened position has geopolitical consequences for the US.

The Way Ahead

The South China Sea has become an important area for the implementation of China's naval strategy, including blockading Taiwan, and power projection into the Indian and Pacific Oceans. It also has some of the busiest shipping lanes in the world.

The Chinese often say that they respect freedom of navigation but can they be trusted? The Japanese think not. During a territorial dispute with Japan in 2010, the Chinese banned the supply of rare earths, which were necessary for Japan's electronics industry, to the country.

The Chinese could block Japanese trade, which would need to be diverted elsewhere at considerable cost. Indeed, control of the South China Sea would allow China to interfere with Japanese and South Korean trade conducted through the area.

For America, then, the future of the current regional order and the security of its allies—Japan and South Korea—is at stake. To maintain its geopolitical position in the western Pacific, the US is obliged to defend the regional alliance system, and reassure local powers who are concerned about China's intentions.

Leaving the South China Sea to the Chinese would undermine that alliance system and America's presence in the western Pacific. China would become the dominant power in the area and regional countries would gravitate towards it.

> The post-war regional order was based on the American presence, which set the stage for impressive economic growth and regional prosperity without the threat of war or conflict.

In October 2015, the Obama Administration responded to China's actions by launching "freedom of navigation" naval patrols in the South China Sea, sending a clear signal that America would not be chased out of the area.

By all indications, the Trump administration is likely to be more aggressive in resisting China in the South China Sea and more forceful about preventing the erosion of America's position in the region.

Trump has already broken with diplomatic convention by speaking with Taiwanese President Tsai Ing-wen over the phone. More can be expected to demonstrate a new American assertiveness.

One possibility is the formation of an American South China Sea naval squadron that would maintain a regular presence in the region to show the Chinese that they cannot dominate the area. The Trump administration might also strengthen security ties with Japan and attempt to orchestrate the creation of a coalition of powers bringing together Australia, India, as well as Japan, to stand up to China.

Print Citations

CMS: Buszynski, Leszek. "Why Is the South China Sea So Important to the US?" In *The Reference Shelf: The South China Sea Conflict*, edited by Betsy Maury, 63-65. Ipswich, MA: H.W. Wilson, 2018.

MLA: Buszynski, Leszek. "Why Is the South China Sea So Important to the US?" *The Reference Shelf: The South China Sea Conflict*. Ed. Betsy Maury. Ipswich: H.W. Wilson, 2018. 63-65. Print.

APA: Buszynski, L. (2018). Why is the South China Sea so important to the US? In Betsy Maury (Ed.), *The reference shelf: The South China Sea conflict* (pp. 63-65). Ipswich, MA: H.W. Wilson. (Original work published 2017)

Japan Is Becoming [a] Player in [the] South China Sea Sovereignty Dispute

By Ralph Jennings
Voa, March 20, 2017

TAIPEI—Japan is building up its influence in the South China Sea, the most widely contested body of water in Asia, to curb Chinese expansion and garner support for its broader military as well as economic interests.

In May, Japan will send its Izumo helicopter-carrying warship to the South China Sea for three months of port visits in Southeast Asia before directing it onward to the Indian Ocean for drills with the United States, according to the U.S. Naval Institute's news website.

"You [will] see this warship more as a multipurpose platform," said Collin Koh, maritime security research fellow at Nanyang Technological University in Singapore. "It can do humanitarian assistance and disaster relief. It can do anti-submarine warfare, so [there are] a few signals Japan wants to send via this deployment."

"Causing Trouble"

Last week, China's foreign ministry spokesperson reacted to word about the warship by urging that Tokyo "refrain from causing trouble in the region" and "respect related countries' efforts to maintain peace and stability," according to the official Xinhua News Agency.

Japan does not claim the South China Sea, a 3.5 million-square-kilometer body of water prized for fisheries and possible undersea fuel reserves.

Six other governments call all or part of it their own, creating friction since the 1960s. Over the past decade China has angered the others by using landfill to expand tiny islets and built military installations on some to fortify its claim to about 95 percent of the sea.

Japan, which does have maritime territorial disputes with Beijing in the East China Sea, will send the ship as part of a longer-term effort to vie with China's influence in Southeast Asian coastal states while cooperating with the United States to bolster a broader power base in Asia, analysts say.

"Like China and the U.S., Japan is trying to consolidate its role as a leader in the region," said Jonathan Spangler, director of the Taipei-based South China Sea

Think Tank. "Part of this effort involves demonstrating that it has the capacity and courage to operate in areas well beyond its own borders."

Island-Building

The United States hopes to stop Chinese island-building in the South China Sea and ensure freedom of navigation, an agenda that has angered Beijing but found a match in Tokyo.

Japan also cares about the safety of undersea communications infrastructure and China's compliance with international laws, Koh said.

Japan and China dispute the eight uninhabited Senkaku Islands in the East China Sea. Analysts say Tokyo's influence in Southeast Asia, along with its close U.S. security relationship, could draw wider sympathy to its Senkaku claim.

> **China and Japan vie for economic influence in Southeast Asia, a hotbed for investment and a vibrant consumer market of about 600 million people.**

Tokyo controls the islets, which are 200 nautical miles (370 kilometers) southeast of Okinawa and called the Diaoyudao in China. It regularly reports spotting Chinese military aircraft flying over nearby waters.

Japan wants to form a "united front" with Southeast Asian countries, said Carl Thayer, emeritus professor of politics at The University of New South Wales in Australia. Brunei, Malaysia, Vietnam and the Philippines contest parts of China's maritime claims in the South China Sea.

"It does not want the Senkakus to be just an isolated incident. Broader context is China's assertiveness and growing power in the Indo-Pacific," he said. "The endgame is stability and getting China to stand down on assertive actions on the Senkakus."

Economic Influence

China and Japan already vie for economic influence in Southeast Asia, a hotbed for investment and a vibrant consumer market of about 600 million people.

Japan has given the region development aid since the 1950s. Last year it pledged to raise the amount. The aid builds political relations while keeping doors open for low-cost investment by Japanese factories.

Vietnam and the Philippines are exploring ways to cooperate with China over the disputed sea, adding urgency for Japan. China offers aid and investment to much of Southeast Asia as well.

Japan's foreign ministry said last year it hoped China would "comply with" a July 2016 world arbitration court ruling against the Chinese claim to about 95 percent of the sea. The Philippines had filed for the arbitration. China rejected the ruling.

"Japan is continuously proactive in terms of providing assistance to the ASEAN (Association of Southeast Asian Nations) countries in terms of conducting ... patrols in the region and also sending the warships to ASEAN countries, very much in line with their emphasis on the rule-based behavior," said Andrew Yang, secretary-general with the Chinese Council of Advanced Policy Studies think tank in Taiwan.

China's dialogue with other countries had "improved" relations in the region, Xinhua said.

Beijing distrusts Japan for what it perceives as an unrepentant stance for its pre-World War Two invasion of mainland China. It also frets over the Japan-U.S. military alliance that U.S. Defense Secretary James Mattis reaffirmed in February.

Japanese Influence

China is used to Japan's influence in Southeast Asia, analysts say.

Japan sent three amphibious ships to the Philippines in 2013 for relief after Typhoon Haiyan killed about 6,300 people in the Southeast Asian country.

Last year, Japan gave the Philippines two patrol vessels and said it would lease training aircraft, adding to an earlier offer of 10 coast guard ships to an otherwise militarily weak nation. Japan agreed in 2014 to sell Vietnam six used maritime surveillance vessels and two months ago pledged to sell it six new patrol ships.

The Chinese foreign ministry spokesperson said Japan "had inflamed the (South China Sea) issue recently, much to the dissatisfaction of the Chinese people," Xinhua reported. Unless Japan shifts direction, the news agency said, "China will definitely respond to any action that harms China's sovereignty and security."

Expect a "continuation" of Japanese military cooperation in Southeast Asia, Thayer said.

Print Citations

CMS: Jennings, Ralph. "Japan Is Becoming [a] Player in [the] South China Sea Sovereignty Dispute." In *The Reference Shelf: The South China Sea Conflict*, edited by Betsy Maury, 66-68. Ipswich, MA: H.W. Wilson, 2018.

MLA: Jennings, Ralph. "Japan Is Becoming [a] Player in [the] South China Sea Sovereignty Dispute." *The Reference Shelf: The South China Sea Conflict*. Ed. Betsy Maury. Ipswich: H.W. Wilson, 2018. 66-68. Print.

APA: Jennings, R. (2018). Japan is becoming [a] player in [the] South China Sea sovereignty dispute. In Betsy Maury (Ed.), *The reference shelf: The South China Sea conflict* (pp. 66-68). Ipswich, MA: H.W. Wilson. (Original work published 2017)

Russia's Tactics and Strategy in the South China Sea

By Anton Tsvetov

Asia Maritime Transparency Initiative, November 1, 2016

Russia's involvement in the South China Sea has historically been marginal. Since withdrawal from Cam Ranh Bay in Vietnam in the early 2000s, Russian military presence has been scarce, though the navy still makes port calls regularly. Russian leaders have not expressed much interest in the ongoing sovereignty disputes, mostly because Russian interest in regional affairs has been relatively weak and limited to maintaining bilateral relations with Northeast Asian states and Vietnam.

Generally, Moscow has taken an explicitly neutral stance on the maritime disputes, usually issued by the foreign minister or the Ministry of Foreign Affairs (MFA) spokesperson. They have repeatedly stated that Russia does not take any sides on sovereignty issues, supports a diplomatic solution, non-use of force, adherence to international law including the United Nations Convention on the Law of the Sea (UNCLOS) and the 2002 Declaration on Conduct, and calls for an early conclusion of negotiations over a binding code of conduct.

Russia has been low-key in the South China Sea because it simply doesn't have much at stake. Little of Russia's energy resources travel through the waters of the South China Sea. Russia does not yet have the reach or need to participate in regional squabbles, and does not have any major economic interests to protect there. Awareness in Russia about the South China Sea is very low, and rarely a matter of presidential politics.

The interest in the disputes that does exist comes from Russia's close ties to both China and Vietnam. Russia is a long-time arms supplier to both countries and has been central to Vietnam's naval modernization, especially with the Vietnamese navy's six Kilo-class submarines capable of carrying Klub missiles. That is in addition to the corvettes, frigates, fighter jets, and missile defense systems that provide Vietnam the capability for retaliation and possibly deterrence against China.

Russia's position between the rivals was expected to become an issue as its political ties with China blossomed after 2014. Both of Russia's partners seem to understand the nature of the dilemma and have generally been very accommodating toward Russian balancing. However, there has been concern in Vietnam that if Russia's economic situation worsens, Russia might fall into over-dependence on China and thereby be leveraged into disposing of its neutrality.

Such fears increased as the July 2016 arbitral ruling on the Philippines' case against China loomed. Observers noticed another bullet-point in Russia's South China Sea stance—the opposition to external interference and, essentially, internationalization of the disputes. This likely stems from Russia's allergic reaction to Western engagement in the post-Soviet space and the traditional criticism of foreign interventions in Yugoslavia, Afghanistan, Iraq, and Libya. However, many saw this as evidence that Russia was leaning toward China.

Another important development came at the G20 Summit in Hangzhou in September 2016, where Russian president Vladimir Putin first publicly stated support for China's defiance of the arbitration ruling. Since then, Russia has spared no effort to reiterate that this addition does not change Russia's neutral stance and does not concern sovereignty or politics. The statement was likely made in view of a similar UNCLOS-based suit that could be soon filed by Ukraine against Russia over the waters surrounding Crimea, and partly in continuation of Russia's non-participation in and non-adherence to an international tribunal on the *Arctic Sunrise* case brought in 2013. Still, the effort to demonstrate continued neutrality indicates that Russia seeks to maintain autonomy from Chinese influence, or at least to look like it is doing so.

> It is fortunate that neither China nor Vietnam have been too assertive in wooing Russia over the South China Sea, because picking either would result in severe diplomatic and reputational damage for Russia.

More recently, Russia and China held joint military drills in the South China Sea bolstering coordination on, among other things, "island-seizing." As menacing as such an exercise may sound, we should be careful in interpreting it as Russian support for China's South China Sea stance. The exercises took place off the coast of Guangdong province, as far from the disputed area as possible while still in the South China Sea. Last year's drills were also held in the controversial waters of the Mediterranean and Black Seas, but far from the Crimean Peninsula. This is why the 2016 drills most likely do not show any change in the level of Russia's support for China, at least not beyond giving Beijing the opportunity to spin the story with headlines like "Russia and China Hold Drills in South China Sea."

Despite these shifts, Russia maintains the same low-profile strategy. At the core of it is a desire to avoid taking sides and maintain an image of power, reach, and independence. It is fortunate that neither China nor Vietnam have been too assertive in wooing Russia over the South China Sea, because picking either would result in severe diplomatic and reputational damage for Russia. Actual participation in any dispute settlement initiatives at this point is also unlikely, as is an increased military presence. Russian politicians, pundits, and government officials speak of "returning" to Cam Ranh Bay from time to time, but it is safe to disregard such proclamations as intended for a domestic audience. Policymakers in the MFA are well-aware of Vietnam's opposition to foreign bases and the low practical benefits of having an actual naval facility in Cam Ranh.

However, the South China Sea will still factor in Russia's grand strategy in Asia, if that strategy takes shape soon. Pivoting to the east, Russia's likely bargaining formula is to sell diplomatic and security capabilities in exchange for economic cooperation. Among Moscow's key talking points in Asia is a call for an inclusive multilateral security architecture. Implementing a project like that would be difficult without taking a more active role in the South China Sea or suggesting a viable approach to untying the knot.

As Russia's Asia policy develops, it is also likely to become more diversified and less focused on China. This trend is manifest in Moscow's 2016 push toward Japan and South Korea, as well as Russia-ASEAN summitry and free-trade ambitions. Will Northeast and Southeast Asian partners ask Russia for a deeper engagement in the South China Sea as another step in their cooperation? They might, and in that case Russia will once again face a tough balancing challenge, with China remaining its number one partner in Asia.

Finally, one of the great issues at stake in the South China Sea is freedom of navigation and the interpretation of this principle. While China does not have meaningful blue water navy capabilities, Russia does, and is actually more inclined toward the U.S. interpretation of what foreign military ships can and cannot do in other states' exclusive economic zones. After all, the 1982 UNCLOS was written by and for global naval powers like Russia.

In the long run, Russia may find itself more deeply involved in the South China Sea, as long as its Asia policy is a full-scale shift and not just a minor change in its bilateral engagements. However, for the time being, while Russian policymakers are still taking the measure of East Asia and merely putting their foot in the door, the main strategy will be to avoid taking sides and getting involved in another geopolitical conundrum like those already abundant in Russia's foreign policy.

Print Citations

CMS: Tsvetov, Anton. "Russia's Tactics and Strategy in the South China Sea." In *The Reference Shelf: The South China Sea Conflict*, edited by Betsy Maury, 69-71. Ipswich, MA: H.W. Wilson, 2018.

MLA: Tsvetov, Anton. "Russia's Tactics and Strategy in the South China Sea." *The Reference Shelf: The South China Sea Conflict*. Ed. Betsy Maury. Ipswich: H.W. Wilson, 2018. 69-71. Print.

APA: Tsvetov, A. (2018). Russia's tactics and strategy in the South China Sea. In Betsy Maury (Ed.), *The Reference Shelf: The South China Sea conflict t* (pp. 69-71). Ipswich, MA: H.W. Wilson. (Original work published 2016)

Philippines Not Married to US, Can Still Pursue China, Says Manila's Top Diplomat

By Catherine Wong
South China Morning Post, July 4, 2017

The Philippines' new foreign secretary, Alan Peter Cayetano, warned that "outside influences" could turn Southeast Asia into "a theatre of geopolitical rivalry" and that Manila's relations with the US should not stop it from forging ties with China.

The 46-year-old made the comment in an interview with the *South China Morning Post*. He is a staunch ally of Duterte and was his vice-presidential running mate. A seasoned politician, Cayetano was reportedly involved in early negotiations with China on a series of multibillion-dollar deals shortly after Duterte was elected last year, according to Philippine media.

Midway through a year in which the Philippines has assumed the rotating chairmanship of Asean, Cayetano said a top challenge for Manila was keeping away external influences in the region.

"Another challenge will be influences from outside the region … making Asean a theatre for what we call geopolitical rivalry," he said. Cayetano did not specify what he meant by outside influences, or whether he was referring to the ongoing competition between China and the US for influence among Asean countries.

Relations between Beijing and Manila have improved significantly since Philippine President Rodrigo Duterte took office last year and promised to put aside territorial disputes in exchange for trade and economic assistance from China.

But Duterte has faced criticism both at home and internationally for being too soft on China over the disputes and has been seen as not having taken full advantage of the landmark tribunal award the Philippines won against China last year.

Manila's rapprochement with Beijing also has been seen as posing a serious test to its traditional alliance with Western powers, including the US.

But Cayetano said Manila's relationship with Washington was not a "marriage" that forbade it from pursuing close relations with other countries, such as China.

As the Philippines holds the chair of Asean this year, the country has come under even stronger scrutiny over whether it can balance its growing ties with China with the interests of other Southeast Asian claimant states.

"It's difficult to balance when you yourself are a claimant," the top Philippine diplomat said. "This means now that our president wears two hats: that of the president of Philippines but also that of the chair of Asean."

But Cayetano said Manila would prioritise the goal of peace and stability in the region over individual nations' interests.

He defended the Duterte administration's decision to put aside the tribunal ruling to seek greater trade with China. The Philippines actually has reinforced its claim over the disputed Scarborough Shoal by reaching fisheries and coastguard agreements with Beijing thanks to warmer ties between the countries, he said.

> **Manila's rapprochement with Beijing also has been seen as posing a serious test to its traditional alliance with Western powers, including the US.**

"People might not agree with this strategy (of putting aside territorial disputes in exchange for trade and economic assistance from China). But it is furthest from the truth to say that we have not capitalised on the victory," Cayetano said.

The tentative fisheries and coastguard agreements reached in October covering the Scarborough Shoal, where the Philippines maintain's a small garrison within view of a newly constructed Chinese naval base and airfield, as well as the reduced risk of military confrontation, were proof that the Duterte administration had adopted the right strategy of dealing with Beijing, Cayetano said.

The fishery agreement allows Philippine fishermen access to the Scarborough Shoal. The coastguard agreement led to the formation of a Joint Coastguard Committee on Maritime Cooperation and reciprocal visits between the two nations' coastguards are scheduled for later this year.

As China and Asean move closer to completing a framework for a code of conduct in the disputed waters, some Asean diplomats and observers have expressed concern over whether the two sides can reach a binding code of conduct that curbs China's efforts to reclaim and militarise other islands in the South China Sea.

But Cayetano cautioned against any attempts to "simplify" the discussions or view an agreement strictly as a legal framework.

"In diplomacy, you look at the direction and the momentum," he said. "So if the direction is that the relationship is getting worse, it doesn't matter what legal mechanism you have, what laws you have passed, because bad relations will just lead you [to] finger pointing … and then to armed conflict and other kinds of conflicts and a world war will erupt."

In the final months of the US presidency of Barack Obama, Duterte went on a tirade against the Obama administration's criticism of the Philippine leader's deadly anti-drugs campaign. Cayetano suggested that Manila still had a wait-and-see attitude towards Obama's successor, Donald Trump, who will visit the Philippines in November for a summit with Southeast Asian leaders.

"We look forward to working with [Trump's] administration," Cayetano said. "And let's see what the [US] policy towards the region and Asean will be."

During his first trip to China as foreign minister—and third since Duterte took power in June last year—Cayetano met his Chinese counterparts State Councillor Yang Jiechi and Foreign Minister Wang Yi, as well as Premier Li Keqiang.

Wang, who said the two countries had entered a "golden period" in their relations, told a joint press conference with Cayetano that China had become the Philippines' biggest trading partner for the first time, and that Beijing strongly supported Duterte's fight against drugs and terrorism.

"China has supported us early on in all aspects of our fight against illegal drugs," said Cayetano, citing Beijing's decision last year to provide funding for a rehabilitation centre for Duterte's anti-drugs campaign.

"[China has also] supported us [before] the Human Rights Council in the UN, while there are some countries who chose to view our problem from their point of view and have refused to believe that there is a connection between illegal drugs or narcotics and terrorism," he said.

China on Wednesday delivered an unspecified consignment of military equipment, worth about 50 million yuan (US$7.4 million), to Manila to help its fight against an Islamist siege in the southern city of Marawi on Mindanao.

Cayetano said the assistance clearly demonstrated the political trust between the two countries as they deepen their cooperation on intelligence sharing and military training against terrorism.

"Since China has been gracious enough in many, many fields of cooperation without conditions, it has really sparked mutual trust," he said.

Print Citations

CMS: Wong, Catherine. "Philippines Not Married to US, Can Still Pursue China, Says Top Diplomat." In *The Reference Shelf: The South China Sea Conflict*, edited by Betsy Maury, 72-74. Ipswich, MA: H.W. Wilson, 2018.

MLA: Wong, Catherine. "Philippines Not Married to US, Can Still Pursue China, Says Top Diplomat." *The Reference Shelf: The South China Sea Conflict*. Ed. Betsy Maury. Ipswich: H.W. Wilson, 2018. 72-74. Print.

APA: Wong, C. (2018). Philippines not married to US, can still pursue China, says top diplomat. In Betsy Maury (Ed.), *The reference shelf: The South China Sea conflict* (pp. 72-74). Ipswich, MA: H.W. Wilson. (Original work published 2017)

Indonesia, Long on Sidelines, Starts to Confront China's Territorial Claims

By Joe Cochrane
The New York Times, September 10, 2017

JAKARTA, Indonesia—When Indonesia recently—and quite publicly—renamed the northernmost waters of its exclusive economic zone in the South China Sea despite China's claims to the area, Beijing quickly dismissed the move as "meaningless."

It is proving to be anything but.

Indonesia's increasingly aggressive posture in the region—including a military buildup in its nearby Natuna Islands and the planned deployment of naval warships—comes as other nations are being more accommodating to China's broad territorial claims in the South China Sea.

The two countries had three maritime skirmishes in 2016 involving warning shots, including one in which Indonesian warships seized a Chinese fishing boat and its crew.

Indonesia is challenging China, one of its biggest investors and trading partners, as it seeks to assert control over a waterway that has abundant resources, particularly oil and natural gas reserves and fish stocks.

The pushback from Indonesia takes direct aim at Beijing's claims within the so-called "nine-dash line," which on Chinese maps delineates the vast area that China claims in the South China Sea. It also adds a new player to the volatile situation, in which the United States Navy has been challenging China's claims with naval maneuvers through waters claimed by Beijing.

Indonesia "is already a party to the disputes—and the sooner it acknowledges this reality the better," said Ian J. Storey, a senior fellow at the Institute of Southeast Asian Studies in Singapore, where he researches South China Sea issues.

The dispute largely centers on the Natuna Sea, a resource-rich waterway north of Indonesia that also lies close to Vietnam's exclusive economic zone.

Before naming part of the contested waterway the North Natuna Sea "to make it sound more Indonesian," Mr. Storey said, Indonesia last year began beefing up its military presence in the Natunas. That included expanding its naval port on the main island to handle bigger ships and lengthening the runway at its air force base there to accommodate larger aircraft.

For decades, Indonesia's official policy has been that it is not a party to any territorial disputes with China in the South China Sea, unlike its regional neighbors Brunei, Malaysia, the Philippines and Vietnam. Last year, however, Indonesia and China had the three maritime skirmishes within Indonesia's 200-nautical-mile exclusive economic zone off its Natuna Islands, which lie northwest of Borneo.

After the third skirmish, in June 2016, China's Ministry of Foreign Affairs issued a statement in which it claimed for the first time that its controversial nine-dash line included "traditional fishing grounds" within Indonesia's exclusive economic zone.

The administration of the Indonesian president, Joko Widodo, whose top administrative priorities since taking office in October 2014 include transforming his country into a maritime power, has ordered the authorities to blow up hundreds of foreign fishing vessels seized while illegally fishing in Indonesian waters.

Mr. Joko, during a visit to Japan in 2015, said in a newspaper interview that China's nine-dash line had no basis in international law. He also chaired a cabinet meeting on a warship off the Natunas just days after last year's third naval skirmish—a move analysts viewed as a show of resolve to Beijing.

On July 14, Indonesia's Ministry of Maritime Affairs and Fisheries held a conspicuously high-profile news conference to release its first national territorial map since 2005, including the unveiling of the newly named North Natuna Sea. The new map also included new maritime boundaries with Singapore and the Philippines, with which Indonesia had concluded agreements in 2015.

> **Indonesia is challenging China, one of its biggest investors and trading partners, as it seeks to assert control over a waterway that has abundant resources, particularly oil and natural gas reserves and fish stocks.**

Arif Havas Oegroseno, a deputy minister at Indonesia's Coordinating Ministry of Maritime Affairs, told journalists that the new Indonesian map offered "clarity on natural resources exploration areas."

That same day, Indonesia's Armed Forces and Ministry of Energy and Mineral Resources signed a memorandum for warships to provide security for the highly profitable fishing grounds and offshore oil and gas production and exploration activities within the country's exclusive economic zone near the Natunas.

Gen. Gatot Nurmantyo, the commander of the Indonesian Armed Forces, said at the time that offshore energy exploration and production activities "have often been disturbed by foreign-flagged vessels"—which some analysts took as a reference to China.

Although several countries take issue with China's territorial claims in the South China Sea, few do so publicly, and the Trump administration has recently sent mixed signals about how willing it is to challenge China on its claims. That has made the Indonesian pushback more intriguing.

Frega Ferdinand Wenas Inkiriwang, a lecturer at the Indonesian Defense University, said Indonesia's public naming of the North Natuna Sea "means that

Indonesia indirectly becomes a claimant state in the area, perhaps due to territorial integrity issues."

"It's in the vicinity of the Natunas," he said, "and the Natunas contain natural resources which are inherited and will be beneficial for Indonesia's development."

Analysts say that the Indonesian Navy would be no match for the Chinese Navy in a fight, although the first of last year's clashes involved only a Chinese Coast Guard ship and an Indonesian maritime ministry patrol boat. It is unlikely that the two countries' navies would clash within Indonesia's exclusive economic zone, according to analysts.

Members of the 10-state Association of Southeast Asian Nations, or Asean, have repeatedly expressed concern about China's aggressive posture in the South China Sea, including its naval standoffs and land reclamation projects in disputed areas, and the stationing of military personnel and surface-to-air missiles in the Paracel Islands—which are controlled by China but are also claimed by Taiwan and Vietnam.

Indonesia, the grouping's largest member and de facto leader, had in the past remained on the sidelines of the various South China Sea disputes and offered to help mediate between Asean claimant states and Beijing.

Given that China is among Indonesia's biggest investors and trade partners, some analysts say Jakarta will go only so far in challenging China's territorial claims, at least publicly. But its more aggressive military posture and other moves regarding the Natunas are nonetheless sending signals to China.

"It doesn't make Indonesia a claimant state," said Aaron Connelly, a research fellow at the Lowy Institute for International Policy in Sydney, Australia, who follows the South China Sea disputes. "They've never accepted the legitimacy of the nine-dash line, which is why they say there's no overlap" with its exclusive economic zone.

"China says it has 'traditional fishing rights,' but Indonesia is doing things in a legalistic way right now," Mr. Connelly said. "This is a more effective way of challenging it."

Evan A. Laksmana, a senior researcher on security affairs at the Center for Strategic and International Studies in Jakarta, agreed that the naming of the North Natuna Sea was not specifically done to trigger a dispute with China.

"But the international legal basis underpinning Indonesia's new map is clear," he said.

"We do not recognize China's claims in the Natuna waters—we don't feel like we should negotiate our map with Beijing or ask their consent," Mr. Laksmana said.

Print Citations

CMS: Cochrane, Joe. "Indonesia, Long on Sidelines, Starts to Confront China's Territorial Claims." In *The Reference Shelf: The South China Sea Conflict*, edited by Betsy Maury, 75-78. Ipswich, MA: H.W. Wilson, 2018.

MLA: Cochrane, Joe. "Indonesia, Long on Sidelines, Starts to Confront China's Territorial Claims." *The Reference Shelf: The South China Sea Conflict*. Ed. Betsy Maury. Ipswich: H.W. Wilson, 2018. 75-78. Print.

APA: Cochrane, J. (2018). Indonesia, long on sidelines, starts to confront China's territorial claims. In Betsy Maury (Ed.), *The reference shelf: The South China Sea conflict* (pp. 75-78). Ipswich, MA: H.W. Wilson. (Original work published 2017)

Malaysia's Special Role in the South China Sea

By Ho Yi Jian
Penang Monthly, October, 2014

In May this year, Chinese oil company China National Offshore Oil Corporation placed the HYSY-981 oil drilling platform approximately 130 nautical miles from the Vietnamese shore. This caused simmering anti-Chinese sentiment to boil over into riots; Chinese and other Asian-owned factories were torched in business parks in Binh Duong, Dong Nai and Ha Tinh provinces in Vietnam. The Vietnamese government acted to quell the riots to protect its relationship with China, and it was not surprising that at a public diplomacy forum in Singapore—the Shangri-La Dialogue in early June—the Chinese government drew flak from the US and Japan, and also a guarded censure from the Vietnamese[1]. While HYSY- 981 was announced to have completed its mission in mid-July, one can only speculate if it was withdrawn for purely operational and technical reasons, or if international pressure had contributed to this in any way.

Such episodes are one of many in a long-running series of maritime disputes about China's claim of "indisputable sovereignty" over most of the South China Sea. Beijing's "nine-dotted line" claims 95% of the area and encompasses clusters of islets and reefs such as the Paracel Islands and Spratly Islands—once deemed mere navigational features but which now have economic, political and security significance. For Malaysia, the challenge lies in that the Chinese claim comes within tens of miles of the Sarawakian coastline. This claim has been promulgated since 1959, when China published an official map of China. As it is, the maritime border disputes involve four Asean states and China.

The placement of HYSY-981 should be a deep concern for Malaysia—perhaps a portent of things to come. Among many of Malaysia's interests in the South China Sea, the most strategically important is the area disputed with China off northern Sarawak and northeast of Sabah which holds significant oil and gas reserves, some in which drilling platforms are currently operating. It's a very severe dispute—Malaysian oil and gas acreage maps can run to 400km into the South China Sea, but the nine-dotted line comes up to 37km off the coast of Sarawak[2]. The East Malaysian oil and gas fields are extremely vital to our economic and energy security especially since our reserves off the coast of Terengganu and Pahang are fast maturing and depleting.

As such, the government will not be able to take encroachment lightly—dividends and payments from Petronas are a substantial portion of federal revenue.

Malaysian Exceptionalism

For the entire region, the lack of clarity over Chinese intentions and their growing military shadow instill fear of a gradually encroaching regional predator. In this regard, Malaysia is not an exception and the country has had incidences with China which are cause for concern. In 2009, Malaysia made a joint submission with Vietnam to the UN Commission on Limits of the Continental Shelf to extend its exclusive economic zone (EEZ) farther into the South China Sea, but this was heavily resisted by the Chinese government, which in reaction sent a *note verbale* with a map of the nine-dotted line. More recent incidents occurred last year in January, when a small flotilla of four PLA Navy ships held an oath-taking ceremony at James Shoal (Beting Serupai/Zengmu reef) in the Spratly Islands. James Shoal sits 80km off Bintulu and Malaysia operates some of its oil and gas platforms in the surrounding waters.

However, Malaysia differs from Vietnam and the Philippines in two salient ways. First, we have less public sentiment entrenched in our South China Sea holdings; Malaysia's interests are extremely economic. Our hydrocarbon exploitation in the South China Sea has been a vital part in our economy, unlike the case for the Filipino and Vietnamese economies.

In contrast, there is greater public sentiment over the symbolic sovereignty Vietnam lost over the Paracel Islands since 1974. While historically there have been great strides in bilateral relations in settling their land border as well as joint development in the Gulf of Tonkin after the 1979 Sino-Soviet War, settling the sovereignty over the Paracels Islands remains a difficult issue. China has consolidated its control over the islands by building Sansha City, a small administrative capital, and in 2012 designating it as the seat of government over the Paracels and Spratly islands. The Vietnamese protested, as expected. The same can be said for the Philippines, which claims some of the Spratly Islands. During the Arroyo government, a 2005 agreement with China, called the Joint Maritime Survey Undertaking (JMSU) to jointly survey the sea, was heavily criticised by public groups as "selling out to China". The agreement was not renewed after three years. A standoff between Chinese and Filipino vessels at Scarborough Shoal in 2012, where Chinese fishing vessels quickly returned to the shoal after a negotiated retreat, left the Philippine government uneasy.

Second, Malaysia has the unique position of having extremely good relations with both the West and the East. The Philippines sits close with the West as they are a formal alliance partner with the US and, driven by their insecurity with China, recently reopened Subic Bay and Clark Air Base for US naval use after having closed it in 1992. On the other hand, due to its communist roots, modern Vietnam sits closer to the East and is only beginning to open up to the West. While it announced its relationship to be a "comprehensive strategic partner" of China in 2009, it seemed to also hedge Chinese domination by opening the historic Cam

Ranh Bay base to foreign navies in 2010. Malaysia's relation with China is one of amicability which in recent years has grown to unprecedented levels. For starters, Malaysia was the first Asean state to recognise the People's Republic of China as a sovereign state in 1974, with Tun Abdul Razak making the inaugural state visit to normalise relations and negotiate cessation of Chinese support for the Communist Party of Malaya. Further deepening of the ties with the Chinese were made by former Prime Minister Tun Abdullah Ahmad Badawi and current Prime Minister Datuk Seri Najib Tun Razak's both making China the destination for their first overseas state visits, and within months of their appointment as prime ministers. A slew of joint memorandums and cooperative agreements with Malaysia were signed in the mid-2000s. In addition, while Chinese trade with Malaysia rose exponentially in the 1990s, it was in 2003 that China really began to join the ranks of our top trading partners. Today, they are Malaysia's top import and export destination, beating Singapore as the foremost export destination in 2011.

Unlike Vietnam and the Philippines, Malaysian actions in disputed waters have been muted – perhaps indicative of the goodwill already built up with the Chinese government. In 1992, the Yang di-Pertuan Agong Sultan Azlan Shah visited Terumbu Layang-layang in the Spratly Islands, about 160 nautical miles off Kota Kinabalu. In 1999, Malaysia also erected structures on Terumbu Peninjau and Terumbu Siput in the Spratly Islands. The occasional promotion of acreage blocks for hydrocarbon development (such as the trading of blocks CA1 and CA2 to Brunei and SK-303B, SK-304A, DWF and DW2) within the disputed area was also met with muted public response from the Chinese government, when compared to the Philippines or Vietnam.

Recent years have been good for relations as well—Chinese President Xi Jinping made a visit to Malaysia last year, and this, among other agreements for further trade and investment deals, culminated in arrangements for joint military exercises and the formalisation of Malaysia as a "comprehensive strategic partner". Xiamen University will open its first overseas branch in Malaysia and will establish a China-Asean Ocean College using funds from the China-Asean Maritime Cooperation Fund[3]. Najib made an official state visit in June this year, and China reciprocated with "panda diplomacy"—a loan of two pandas. Our relationship with China seems so strong that in reaction to the James Shoal incident, Defence Minister Hishammuddin Hussein said that "we will not be moved by day-to-day politics or emotions"[4], and in a separate international forum, Najib praised China for its "restraint"[5].

The Strategic Environment/Constraints

There are at least three strategic considerations over Chinese intent, vague as they may be. First, rising China brings to the table its own cultural and historical baggage. Sinologists often point towards internalised Chinese "victim mentality" for the "century of humiliation" stretching from the Opium War to the end of World War II. Extremely sensitive of foreign intervention, "core interests" Xinjiang, Tibet and Taiwan are top priorities for China in maintaining its territorial integrity against further colonial influence. We are lucky that the South China Sea has not been formally designated as a "core interest" and the Chinese are at least rhetorically willing to negotiate with South-East Asian nations at a bilateral level.

Second, the Chinese are dealing with their newfound economic power, progressively building their military power to be proportionate to what they perceive to be a historically denied great power status. Recognising the abrasion a rising power causes to existing order, the Xi Jinping government promulgated a "New Security Concept" where Hu Jintao's government was marked by his concept of "Harmonious World". These represented efforts to stress peaceful development. At the same time, the Chinese government is also extremely fearful of Western conspiracies that aim to build coalitions to contain its rise.

Finally, it is trying to deal with its own resource scarcity and economic security. The South China Sea contains vital sea lines of communication, rich fishery stock (news occasionally surfaces of Chinese fishing vessels detained by Vietnamese or Filipino vessels), as well as a moderate amount of hydrocarbon resources which it could use to secure its ever-increasing energy needs.

While Chinese foreign policy is perceived to have taken an assertive turn since 2008, at the very least the situation in the South China Sea has not spiralled out of control. The standoffs have not escalated into military naval encounters as vessels on both sides are hesitant about opening fire and are more likely to ram each other or blast water-cannons. Chinese vessels tend rather to be from the paramilitary coast guard than PLA Navy warships.

The US stand remains relatively non-committal. While the Obama administration has announced a rebalance to Asia, US statements on the South China Sea remain restrained and hard-won. After fighting two wars in Iraq and Afghanistan, it hardly wants to have to pick sides with its Asian allies against China, which holds a great deal of its treasury bonds and is a major trade partner. In 2010, it seemed that the Vietnamese managed to win a concession from US Secretary of State Hillary Clinton who announced that the US is invested in the freedom of navigation in the South China Sea. The US has also vacillated on military support for the Philippines should China use forceful action in the Spratly Islands.

In addition, the Chinese are often abrasive when the US is called in to mediate, and see US support as a moral hazard for the Philippines and Vietnam. However, there have been at-sea incidents between the US and China in the South China Sea and they seem committed to keeping these incidents under wraps.

Opportunities for Malaysia

While it may look as if Asean is a natural leverage for Malaysia, there are several structural problems that hinder an Asean-led solution. First is China's insistence that the disputes are strictly bilateral. Secondly, because Asean operates on consensus, it is easy for a single member state to scuttle discussions for the whole; Cambodia for example acceded to China's request to take South China Sea discussions out of the agenda at the Asean summit during its chairmanship in 2012. The lack of depth in Asean's economic and social cooperation means that it will be difficult for Asean to have both the political and identity suasion to keep all its members in line. Even though Asean has been searching for a Code of Conduct at least since 1992 and reaffirmed this again in 2002 through the "Declaration on the Conduct of Parties in the South China Sea", we have seen little progress in negotiations, and proactivity from the Philippines and Indonesia seems to have been met with a weak response.

All this could culminate in 2015, which could prove pivotal for Malaysia to push for a deeper resolution of the South China Sea disputes. Malaysia next year takes on the mantle of Asean chairmanship from Myanmar and will be in charge of finalising the implementation of the Asean Economic Community whose deadline is the end of next year. Malaysia is also lobbying for a non-permanent seat at the UN Security Council for 2015.

With increased exposure on the international stage, it is conceivable that Malaysia will gain a lot of goodwill from China, if only to use the momentum and exposure Malaysia would possess, to drive existing mechanisms. On the one hand, Najib recognised the issue by mentioning after his June 2014 visit to China that both countries are committed to finding a negotiated solution[6]. On the other, he has also said that China has not offered Malaysia a mediation role as "we have not reached that level"[7].

Given such a position and given the political capital built up with China and the West, Malaysia should seize the political window. One method would be to bolster the Chinese discursive bandwagon. Chinese strategic language of "peaceful rise" is less than persuasive in the Western world. Malaysia could start by emphasising the common post-colonial background it has with China and the common commitment to legitimate economic growth,

> **It's a very severe dispute—Malaysian oil and gas acreage maps can run to 400km into the South China Sea, but the nine-dotted line comes up to 37km off the coast of Sarawak.**

but also demonstrate that further antagonism in the South China Sea serves only to damage their own rhetoric of harmony and peaceful rise. If the trust between both countries is as high as it looks, this could persuade China to move towards a Code of Conduct in the South China Sea and eventually work towards a resolution acceptable to Malaysia and Asean on the status of sovereignty in the South China Sea.

If Malaysia should side further with China, it still has to position itself as a neutral power in order not to be seen as a client state and lose credibility with other claimant states as well as the US. The weakness of the Malaysian leadership will likely be in its influence on Vietnam and the Philippines; extra care will have to be taken not to damage their own sense of national pride and national interests. The Philippines has forged ahead with its own case to the Permanent Court of Arbitration in The Hague on the legitimacy of the "nine-dotted line" claim[8]. But Malaysia has cooperated with Vietnam and the Philippines in related cases, such as its role in mediating the Mindanao peace treaty and the joint submission with Vietnam of the 2009 UN Commission on the Limits of the Continental Shelf.

Other related factors may also become relevant. During the most recent Asean Summit in Nay Pyi Taw, Chinese Foreign Minister Wang Yi said that the Declaration of Conduct was "the truly effective approach to maintain peace and stability in the South China Sea"; a special China-Asean Senior Officials Meeting was held in September; and the 12th Joint Working Group Meeting on the implementation of the Declaration of Conduct will be held in October in Thailand. News have also surfaced that China and the US are also beginning to talk about a Code of Conduct after an incident with US surveillance planes in the South China Sea, in the hope that the terms could set a precedent for Asean[9]. Even Joko Widodo, Indonesia's president-elect, has offered to act as an intermediary in the South China Sea disputes[10]. As the next Asean Chair, Malaysia should leverage on all endorsing factors to keep the diplomatic momentum going and to ensure that negotiations at all levels do not stall.

Rising Prominence

While a Code of Conduct will be a landmark victory for all sides, the larger goal should be an agreement on sovereignty issues in the South China Sea. While the negotiated end point may not be completely optimal for all nations, Malaysia could make a historically important mark in the qualitative security environment next year. But to do that, it will have to push for more to be done, despite the competing need to make the fast-approaching deadline for the Asean Economic Community to be fully implemented by the end of 2015.

At the regional level, Chinese reactions towards the Philippines' arbitration case on the nine-dotted line will prove pivotal as it demonstrates how China will react towards international law even though it publicly rejects arbitration. Malaysia needs to weigh in on that too.

Notes

1. https://www.iiss.org/en/publications/conference%20proceedings/sections/shangri-la-aa36/theshangri-la-dialogue-2014-f844/sld14-07-plenary-3-bbe0
2. Author's estimate.
3. www.whatsonxiamen.com/news35105.html
4. See http://thediplomat.com/2014/03/speak-softly-and-carry-a-big-stick-what-is-malaysia-playingat/, although Hishamuddin's comments were then retracted by ministry officials as not being reflective of policy, it does reflect the general sentiment of the political leadership towards China.
5. "Stirring up the South China Sea (II): Regional Responses", International Crisis Group, Brussels, 2012, p.11.
6. www.thestar.com.my/News/ Nation/2014/06/02/Firm-on-negotiatedsolution/
7. www.themalaymailonline.com/malaysia/article/najib-describes-china-trip-as-encouraging-fordiplomatic- relations
8. www.pca-cpa.org/showpage.asp?pag_id=1529
9. http://english.cntv.cn/2014/08/29/ VIDE1409266081922401.shtml

10. www.channelnewsasia.com/news/asiapacific/indonesia-ready-to/1308176. html

Print Citations

CMS: Ho Yi Jian. "Malaysia's Special Role in the South China Sea." In *The Reference Shelf: The South China Sea Conflict*, edited by Betsy Maury, 79-85. Ipswich, MA: H.W. Wilson, 2018.

MLA: Ho Yi Jian. "Malaysia's Special Role in the South China Sea." *The Reference Shelf: The South China Sea Conflict*. Ed. Betsy Maury. Ipswich: H.W. Wilson, 2018. 79-85. Print.

APA: H.Y. Jian. (2018). Malaysia's special role in the South China Sea. In Betsy Maury (Ed.), *The reference shelf: The South China Sea conflict* (pp. 79-85). Ipswich, MA: H.W. Wilson. (Original work published 2014)

4
Environmental Concerns

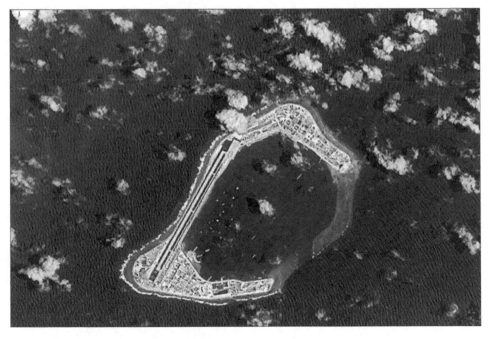

Photo by USGS/NASA Landsat data/Orbital Horizon/Gallo Images/Getty Images

A satellite image of Subi Reef, an artificial island being developed by China in the Spratly Islands in the South China Sea. Image taken 4 September 2016.

Protecting Oceanic Environments

With so many overlapping territorial, political, and diplomatic issues at play, the environmental impact of the South China Sea military and developmental buildup is often overlooked. Environmental studies of the South China Sea have found that fishing, the harvest of petroleum products, and China's dredging to create artificial islands, have collectively resulted in vast environmental destruction. The ecoregion of the South China Sea encompasses hundreds of islands, rocks, cays, banks, reefs, shoals, and atolls concentrated in the sea's three archipelagos. Environmental scientists have noted that little is known about the ecosystems of the region, but that the current political impasse, and failure of China to adhere to United Nations Convention on the Law of the Sea (UNCLOS) environmental restrictions, has resulted in a rapid decline in environmental quality and sustainability.

Diversity of the South China Sea

The hundreds of oceanic features within the South China Sea are concentrated around the sea's three major archipelagos, the Pratas (also known as Dungsha), the Paracels (Xisha), and the Spratly Islands (Nansha), which is the largest of the three.

Pratas Island, which is the northernmost feature of the sea, is an entirely sand-based island (with no soil and little vegetation), approximately 1.7 sq km across and containing a large (0.6 km) lagoon. The Paracel Islands are located between Vietnam and the Philippines, and consist of several small islands and reefs. The Spratly Islands contain 150 named landforms and more than 600 submerged reefs. All three island groups are subjected to similar atmospheric conditions, with subtropical marine climate and monsoons between March and April and from May to November. While a few of the islands have fresh water, most do not and, given the strong winds, long dry season, and scarcity of soil, vegetation is sparse throughout. Some of the larger islands support small tropical forests, scrub forests, mangrove forests, and/or coastal grassland habitats. Scientists have discovered 340 species of plant and fungi living on the islands, including 312 species of flowering plants, 5 species of fern, one species of lichen, and 22 species of fungi. Plants like coconut, papaya, banana, peach, and palm have been cultivated on the islands, and there have been no comprehensive studies of botanical biodiversity.

The few studies conducted of the South China Sea archipelagos suggest that the islands are essential habitat for the green turtle (*Chelonia mydas*) and the hawksbill turtle (*Eretmochelys imbricate*). Historical records indicate that both species once occurred in large numbers, though numbers have decreased due to hunting, pollution, and global warming. Several seabird species, including the brown booby (*Sula leucogaster*), red-footed booby (*Sula sula*), white tern (*Gygis alba*), and the shearwater (*Calonectris leucomelas*) use the islands for resting, breeding, and wintering, though the biodiversity of birds on the island has not been effectively studied.[1]

Efforts to estimate marine diversity in the South China Sea have been more extensive. Studies of marine life began in the 1950s, through China's Qingdao Marine Biological Laboratory. As of 2018, scientists have recorded 22,629 marine species in 46 different phyla. This includes 3,365 species of marine fishes living in and around the reefs and other features.

Among the many different microenvironments in the sea are tidal bays, coral reefs, shoals, seamounts, mangrove forests, and a field of seagrass that was once extensive but is now considered critically threatened.[2] The reefs themselves contain 500 species of reef-building corals, making the South China Sea among the world's most diverse reef ecosystems. Reefs in the Caribbean, by way of comparison, contain only 70 species of corals. Other studies have shown that the South China Sea was at one time home to 10 species of true sea snakes and innumerable marine invertebrates. Despite years of concerted study by international scientists, the biodiversity of the region remains largely unexplored and new species are regularly found by survey programs. A Chinese research program in 2016, for instance, revealed a previously unknown species of seahorse (*Hippocampus casscsio sp.*) living among the threatened seagrass beds in Beibu Bay off the coast of Vietnam.[3] By some estimates, the sea may be home to more than 76 percent of the world's coral species and 37 percent of reef fish species, making the South China Seas one of the world's richest underwater ecosystems.

The Resources of the Sea

The ocean has always been a profound source of food and other resources for humanity. Seafood forms a major part of the diet in many countries, and the seas and oceans have yielded a plethora of other profitable crops and products that play a major role in economies of nations around the world. More recently, the discovery of oceanic petroleum deposits has created a new level of economic value to marine territories. The oil deposits in the South China Sea are believed to be vast and thus, as the nations of the world struggle in the ultimately unsustainable and diminishing petroleum industry, the existence of such reserves has intensified the territorial debate.

One of the most significant threats to the biodiversity of the South China Sea ecosystem is overfishing. The United Nations estimates that, each decade, 30 percent of the South China Sea seagrass habitat, 16 percent of the mangrove forests, and 16 percent of the region's live coral habitat, is destroyed due to harvesting and other unsustainable use. Fisheries within the region support 270 million people and the gradual decline of fish populations has already devastated the economies of many coastal communities. In an effort to increase their annual harvest and counter the declining supply, fishermen in the region increasingly use explosives and poisons that increase their haul from daily fishing excursions but ultimately hasten the decline of the fisheries. Researchers believe that the sea will lose 9 to 59 percent of fish stocks by 2045 due to overfishing and pollution alone and that climate change will exacerbate and intensify the loss of biodiversity over this period. Ultimately, the South China Sea will no longer be a viable fishing habitat and this will not only devastate the interconnected marine environments for thousands of kilometers around the sea, but will result in food shortages, unemployment, poverty, and social turmoil among the local communities and states that depend on fishing.[4]

In their haste to develop their claimed territories, China's exceedingly irresponsible environmental management has become a primary threat to the region's ecosystems. With military control over many of the Spratly Islands, the region's most important and diverse archipelago, China has failed to prevent ships from harvesting endangered species, including sea turtles. China further allows boats to engage in "propeller chopping," which is a method used to harvest another critically endangered species, the giant clam (*Tridacna gigas*) and this method results in large-scale destruction of the reef environments. In the 2015-2016 UN case between the Philippines and China, part of the court's ruling against China was based on the nation's poor environmental management, a fact that China denies. John McManus, professor of marine ecology at the University of Miami, testified to the tribunal and called the propeller chopping method the most damaging to marine life of anything he'd witnessed in four decades of research. In the final 500-page ruling by the tribunal, they found that Chinese development had resulted in 48 square miles of damaged reef among the Spratly Islands, with China responsible for 99 percent of the damage.[5]

Scientists have stated that there are probably hundreds of thousands of unknown species living in the reefs and other ecosystems and warn that the extinction (local or otherwise) of these species might constitute a far greater loss than is generally understood, in the form of medical knowledge. Many medicines come from substances found in natural tissues, like aspirin—arguably one of the most transformative medical breakthroughs in history—which came from salycilic acid taken from plants in the *Spiraea* group. The development of medicines and from marine species is still in its infancy, but has yielded surprising results. For instance, secosteroids, isolated from corals, are being used to develop treatments for asthma, arthritis, and inflammatory diseases, while promising anticancer compounds have been isolated from marine plants and animals as well, several of which are already in use and constitute one of the most effective current lines of research into curing cancer.[6] Scientist Andrew Bruckner argues—given that 40 to 50 percent of all drugs in use come from natural products, and that 80 percent of all life lives in the oceans—that scientists are 300 to 400 times more likely to discover important new drugs from reef environments than from any other ecosystem.[7]

Building Islands and Harvesting Oil

As part of the political and military machinations of China's nine-dash line policy, China has engaged in a dredging program to build onto the terrestrial surface of some of the Spratly Islands, transforming the windswept rocks into military outposts. The dredging itself disturbs the fragile reef environments, while the change in oceanic currents disrupts cays and lagoons. The environmental impacts of the island building project was one of the subjects considered in The Hague as the UN tribunal weighed arguments regarding the legality of China's territorial claims.[8] Until the release of the Hague's 500-page ruling, it was uncertain how the island-building program had effected the environment. Scientists testifying before the tribunal indicated that the rate of environmental destruction had been far greater than previously imagined. Professor McManus told the panel that the program is the most rapid permanent loss of coral reef in known history. Chinese dredgers have reclaimed nearly 800 hectares (8 sq kilometers) since 2013, while Vietnam has also engaged in reclamation. A study from Singapore released in April found further that other shallow features surrounding the reefs had also been dredged to provide building materials.[9]

In 2017, scientists studying the South China Sea reported that pollution from oil leaks and commercial shipping had affected 3.5 million-square kilometers of the sea environment. As the seaway supports 1/3rd of commercial oceanic shipping, and between 333,000 and 1.6 million fishing vessels, pollution is inevitable and has been building for more than a century. Pollution and the acidification of ocean environments is a global problem, but is far more severe in high traffic shipping routes and whenever petroleum exploration occurs. Experts argue that the political impasse in the region has limited efforts to establish cooperative agreements that might contain environmental measures or might at least enable neighboring nations to work together on conservation measures.[10]

An Incompatible Situation

Reports on the ecology of the South China Sea indicate that, while oil exploration, overfishing, and China's island building activities are all sources of significant environmental damage, the biggest threat to the ecosystems of the South China Sea, and to ocean environments around the world, is climate change. Rising seawater temperatures will kill a vast number of marine species over the coming decades and ocean acidification will deepen this pattern. The world's climate is changing as a result of human-centered activity, and the harvesting of fossil fuels has contributed to this.

Politicians in the United States are not hesitant to criticize China's environmental policies, and this is fitting as the nation contributes 30 percent of the world's greenhouse emissions each year, making it the leading source of pollution in the world. However, with the United States contributing 15 percent of the world's annual greenhouse gas emissions, and with the Trump Administration officially denying the existence of climate change and withdrawing from climate change agreements, the United States has an equally poor record for environmental management.[11] There are no easy ways to cope with climate change. The only realistic method is to invest heavily in alternative, sustainable energy. Unless new modes of energy production like these are embraced by the world's largest and most powerful countries, like China and the United States, the destruction of ecosystems in the

South China Sea will have little impact compared to the environmental catastrophe that is coming.

Micah L. Issitt

Works Used

Bruckner, Andrew W. "Life-Saving Products from Coral Reefs." *Issues in Science and Technology*. Vol. 18, No. 3. 2002. Web. 18 Dec 2017.

Carroll, Clint. "Protecting the South China Sea: Chinese Island-Building and the Environment." *Foreign Affairs*. Council on Foreign Relations, Inc. Jun 9 2017. Web. 18 Dec 2017.

Dennis, Brady, Juliet Eilperin, and Chris Mooney. "Trump Administration Releases Report Finding 'No Convincing Alternative Explanation' for Climate Change." *The Washington Post*. The Washington Post Company. Nov 3 2017. Web. 18 Dec 2017.

"Global Greenhouse Gas Emissions Data." *EPA*. Environmental Protection Agency. 2015. Web. 18 Dec 2017.

Jennings, Ralph. "South China Sea Succumbing to Pollution Due to Political Impasse." *VOA*. VOA News. Sep 12 2017. Web. 18 Dec 2017.

Levins, Nicole. "Coral Reefs Could Hold the Cures for Some of the Human Race's Most Common—and Serious—Ailments." *Nature*. Nature Conservancy. 2017. Web. 18 Dec 2017.

Liu, J.Y. "Status of Marine Biodiversity of the China Seas." *PLoS ONE*. Jan 8 2013. Web. 18 Dec 2017.

Makinen, Julie. "China Has Been Killing Turtles, Coral and Giant Clams in the South China Sea, Tribunal Finds." *Los Angeles Times*. Jul 13 2016. Web. 18 Dec 2017.

"Oil and Gas: Top Recipients." *Opensecrets*. Center for Responsive Politics. 2017. Web. 18 Dec 2017.

"South China Sea, between the Philippines, Borneo, Vietnam, and China." *Worldwildlife*. World Wildlife Fund. 2017. Web. 18 Dec 2017.

"South China Sea Countries to Cooperate on Integrating Fisheries and Marine Ecosystem Management." *UNEP*. United Nations Environment. Nov 1 2016. Web. 18 Dec 2017.

Thomas, Madeleine. "Climate Depression Is for Real: Just Ask a Scientist." *Grist*. Grist Magazine Inc. Oct 28 2014. Web. 18 Dec 2017.

Torode, Greg. "'Paving Paradise': Scientists Alarmed over China Island Building in Disputed Sea." *Reuters*. Reuters Inc. Jun 25 2015. Web. 18 Dec 2017.

Wang, Jennifer. "Trump's Stock Portfolio: Big Oil, Big Banks and More Foreign Connections." *Forbes*. Forbes Inc. Nov 29 2016. Web. 18 Dec 2017.

Zhang, Y.H., G. Qin, X. Wang, and Q. Lin. "A New Species of Seahorse (*Teleostei: Syngnathidae*) from the South China Sea." *Zootaxa*. Sep 23, 2016. Web. 18 Dec 2017.

Notes

1. "South China Sea," *Worldwildlife*.
2. Liu, "Status of Marine Biodiversity of the China Seas."
3. Zhang, et al., "A New Species of Seahorse (*Teleostei: Syngnathidae*) from the South China Sea."
4. "South China Sea Countries to Cooperate on Integrating Fisheries and Marine Ecosystem Management," *UNEP*.
5. Makinen, "China Has Been Killing Turtles, Coral and Giant Clams in the South China Sea, Tribunal Finds."
6. Levins, "Coral Reefs Could Hold the Cures for Some of the Human Race's Most Common—and Serious—Ailments."
7. Bruckner, "Life-Saving Products from Coral Reefs."
8. Carroll, "Protecting the South China Sea: Chinese Island-Building and the Environment."
9. Torode, "'Paving Paradies': Scientists Alarmed over China Island Building in Disputed Sea."
10. Jennings, "South China Sea Succumbing to Pollution Due to Political Impasse."
11. "Global Greenhouse Gas Emissions Data," *EPA*.

One Result of China's Buildup in South China Sea: Environmental Havoc

By Jackie Northam
NPR, September 1, 2016

Just over a month ago, the Permanent Court of Arbitration in The Hague issued two important rulings. One soundly rejected Beijing's extensive claim of sovereignty in the South China Sea. The other focused on whether China had caused environmental damage as it constructed artificial islands in the region to help prop up its claim.

The South China Sea's disputed waters are claimed by seven countries, and The Hague rulings came in response to a case brought against China by the Philippines. China dismissed The Hague's decision as "nothing but a scrap of paper."

But Kent Carpenter, a professor of biological science at Old Dominion University and an expert witness for the tribunal, says The Hague tribunal's findings were nothing short of damning.

"The tribunal clearly decided that China had caused severe harm to the coral reef environment," he says. China also violated its obligations under the United Nations Convention on the Law of the Sea "to preserve and protect fragile ecosystems," he says.

The tribunal found that damage to the coral reefs in the Spratly Islands is extensive, spreading for more than 30 square miles. Much of that damage is caused by China's island-building—turning pristine reefs into permanent military outposts that include massive runways.

John McManus, a professor of marine ecology at the University of Miami, says the Chinese use huge dredgers to pull up sand and anything else in their way.

"They're using a grinding ball," he says. "It's got grooves and teeth and it spins around and tears up living coral and parts of the coral reef substrate, to make more gravel and sand to be sucked up and used for island-building."

The dredgers also create plumes of sediment, McManus says. When it lands, the sediment smothers coral, fish, whole marine ecosystems. He says this has been devastating to one of the world's most biodiverse regions.

"We're talking about some of the highest diversity in the world," he says. "You may have 70 species of coral, roughly, in the Caribbean, about 70 or so in Hawaii—but here, we're talking well over 400 species of coral. And it's the same ratios for fish and invertebrates."

> **Even if China were to abandon the artificial islands, the environment in the area could take decades—if ever—to recover.**

However destructive the island-building is, it's nothing compared to the damage done by the poaching of giant clams, says Carpenter. Chinese fishermen have been destroying entire reefs, he says, by using propellers to try to dredge up and harvest the clams, which appear on the IUCN Red List as a "vulnerable" species.

The fishers anchor a boat, rev up the engine and swing the propeller from side to side, he says. "The action of the propeller basically uncovers and breaks up all of the coral, so that the giant clams are basically easy to extract," he says.

Carpenter says The Hague tribunal found the Chinese government had essentially turned a blind eye to the poaching of giant clams.

The poachers' actions help China back up its claim that it's only building artificial islands on dead coral reefs, not living ones, McManus says.

"So in a way," he says, "China is not lying, they're telling the truth. They actually built on dead coral—because the Chinese fishers had already killed the coral."

Beijing has recently started cracking down on the poachers, he says. But Edgardo Gomez, a marine biologist at the University of the Philippines, says it may be too late.

"There are half-a-dozen species of giant clams in the world that are within that area," he says, "and all of the living clams plus the shells have been virtually wiped out of the South China Sea." The Philippines tried restocking, but the clams were wiped out again.

China was invited to—but did not—provide evidence to The Hague tribunal to back up its claims that it had done extensive environmental studies before constructing islands in the South China Sea. Carpenter says there's concern China will continue to build up islands and destroy the environment.

"If it does, then it will begin to lose all of its credibility with regard to its own international obligations," he says.

Even if China were to abandon the artificial islands, he warns, the environment in the area could take decades—if ever—to recover. Tearing down the islands at this point, he says, isn't the answer, either, and would cause more damage than has already been done.

Print Citations

CMS: Northam, Jackie. "One Result of China's Buildup in South China Sea: Environmental Havoc." In *The Reference Shelf: The South China Sea Conflict*, edited by Betsy Maury, 95-97. Ipswich, MA: H.W. Wilson, 2018.

MLA: Northam, Jackie. "One Result of China's Buildup in South China Sea: Environmental Havoc." *The Reference Shelf: The South China Sea Conflict*. Ed. Betsy Maury. Ipswich: H.W. Wilson, 2018. 95-97. Print.

APA: Northam, J. (2018). One result of China's buildup in South China Sea: Environmental havoc. In Betsy Maury (Ed.), *The reference shelf: The South China Sea conflict* (pp. 95-97). Ipswich, MA: H.W. Wilson. (Original work published 2016)

The Rising Environmental Toll of China's Offshore Island Grab

By Mike Ives

Yale Environment 360, October 10, 2016

In the late 1980s, marine biologist John McManus and his colleagues made a surprising discovery while studying near-shore Philippine reefs in the South China Sea: Some fish species seemed to disappear, only to reappear a year or two later. "We figured they weren't coming from other parts of the coast because the entire South China Sea, with the exception of Brunei, is equally overfished," says McManus, a professor of marine biology and fisheries at the University of Miami.

The researchers' hunch, which proved to be correct, was that larvae were floating to the near-shore reefs from the Spratlys—an offshore archipelago that lies between Vietnam and the Philippines and is a key spawning ground for one of the world's most productive fisheries. Scientists later reported that the South China Sea, which is the size of India and has hundreds of islands and islets, has some of the highest marine biodiversity on earth, with 571 known species of reef corals alone.

But the South China Sea's rich natural heritage, long threatened by overfishing, now faces a new ecological danger: A campaign by China to build artificial islands on disputed reefs in the Spratlys and elsewhere in the sea. China's island-building initiative signals an aggressive stance intended to secure dominance in the South China Sea, a strategic area that contains some of the world's busiest shipping lanes and is a potential source of oil deposits.

Over the past several years, Chinese President Xi Jinping has ordered engineers to pile sand onto some of the sea's disputed offshore reefs, mostly in the Spratlys, with the apparent goal of building military bases there. Satellite imagery shows that China has so far constructed seven artificial islands in the Spratlys, and added ports, radar equipment, and airstrips. Three of the seven islands were designed as military bases, U.S. military officials say, and one has an anchorage larger than Hawaii's Pearl Harbor. Marine scientists worry that the next target for dredging and construction will be Scarborough Shoal off the Philippine coast—which, like the Spratlys, is also known for its rich biodiversity.

Based on satellite information, computer-modeling data, and previous studies of human impacts on coral reefs, scientists are concerned that China's campaign may be causing irreparable damage. Coral reefs in the Spratlys and other offshore regions, including the Paracel Islands and Scarborough Shoal, supply larvae for fisheries that feed hundreds of millions of people. They also are a living seed bank that could help the region's marine communities deal with the long-term impacts of climate change.

The scientists' concerns stem partly from the island-construction process. Ships more than 300 feet long have been dredging deep-water channels and harbors, while smaller boats have dredged in shallower waters around reef flats and lagoons by digging up corals with their propellers, according to a forthcoming study by McManus. Both activities produce plumes of sand and silt that coat living reefs and block their access to sunlight. Deep-water dredging can also lower the existing seafloor by up to 30 feet, the study said, changing wave patterns and inhibiting the growth of the red algae that are essential to reef calcification and sedimentation.

Additional local and regional damage to reefs and fish stocks will occur, scientists say, if China turns some of the new artificial islands on the Spratlys into harbors for the country's commercial fishing fleet.

"What you're essentially talking about is destroying the equivalent of seven worldwide natural heritage areas," says Kent Carpenter, a professor at Old Dominion University in Virginia who has studied coral reefs in the Philippines for four decades.

The long-term environmental impacts of China's activities on the seven Spratly reefs it occupies may never be known unless the Chinese military allows independent experts to conduct research there, scientists say. But nearly six square miles of artificial islands have been built recently on disputed reefs in the sea, primarily in the greater Spratly Islands, according to the McManus study. Vietnam, Malaysia, Taiwan, and the Philippines accounted for just a tiny percentage of that construction, the study said, while China's activities were responsible for 99 percent of the resulting damage to offshore coral reefs.

Although six square miles may seem like a small area, the McManus study indicates that the total damage from island building and dredging has already affected more than 10 percent of the Spratlys' total shallow reef area.

China has long claimed offshore territories in as much as 90 percent of the South China Sea. Its claims overlap with competing ones by Vietnam, the Philippines, and other nations. Tensions over the claims have simmered for decades, and some countries have conducted limited land reclamation work on disputed islands and atolls.

In July, the Philippines won a landmark case at a United Nations tribunal, successfully challenging China's territorial claims in the sea. (Both McManus and Carpenter worked as paid science advisors to the Philippines on the case.) But President Xi has vowed to ignore the tribunal's ruling, and some analysts think that China's island-building efforts could raise geopolitical tensions and eventually lead to military conflict with rival claimants or the United States.

At the center of this drama lie the 12 main islets and more than 100 coral reefs of the Spratlys. Scientists describe the Spratlys as biological "stepping stones" for successive generations of corals and fish, meaning that larvae float hundreds of miles toward the Spratlys on ocean currents and stop in eddies near their corals to breed. Successive generations then travel further to create or repopulate marine communities elsewhere in the South China Sea, the Gulf of Thailand, or the Coral Triangle between Indonesia, the Philippines, and the Solomon Islands.

The Spratlys are "positioned very neatly to transfer biodiversity" across open water, says Clive Wilkinson, the former lead coordinator for the non-profit Global Coral Reef Monitoring Network. In addition to producing larvae, the Spratly reefs also function as biological "roadside cafes" for migratory fish, including tuna, that travel through the South China Sea on their way to the Indian Ocean and stop at the Spratlys to feed, he adds. "So any damage to them [the reefs] will have long-term repercussions," says Wilkinson.

The South China Sea is chronically understudied, in large part because so many of its offshore rocks, reef, and atolls are military-patrolled zones that scientists cannot access. Chou Loke Ming, a coral reef expert at the National University of Singapore, says that nearly all on-the-ground scientific research on the South China Sea has so far been confined to near-shore areas where territorial ownership is not as murky as it is in the Spratlys.

But the existing science already paints a portrait of abundant biodiversity. For example, a 2015 computer-modeling study found that larvae from the coral species *Acropora millepora*, whose intricate branches help to shelter other organisms, float from the Spratlys across large swathes of the South China Sea and the Coral Triangle, "further highlighting the importance of the Spratly Islands to the greater region." And a 2015 species survey said previous estimates of the South China Sea's reef biodiversity have been "exceedingly low," largely because of a lack of data for the Spratlys and some reefs off the Philippine island of Luzon.

> **"You're talking about destroying the equivalent of seven worldwide natural heritage areas," says one expert.**

Scientists think the Spratly reefs' genetic diversity could help them weather the impacts of storms, ocean acidification, and other impacts linked to global warming. Larvae from the reefs could help repopulate distant marine communities that are less biologically resilient. If patches of biodiversity "blink out" occasionally across the South China Sea, "the idea is that if you have a lot of exchange, they'll be re-seeded in the near future," says Eric Treml, a marine biologist at the University of Melbourne who has created computer models of regional fish-larvae movement.

Scientists say China's island building may imperil that system of genetic diversity and biological connectivity. But how great is the cumulative threat from reef building and fishing? McManus estimates that China has already caused 55 square miles of "decadal-scale" damage through giant-clam harvesting and seafloor dredging near its new islands. That is worrying because seafloor dredging can kill corals by blocking their access to sunlight as has happened near Australia's Great Barrier Reef, where sediment plumes extended for up to 28 miles from a seafloor dredging site.

By contrast, only 6.5 square miles of South China Sea reefs have been damaged by China's island building and dredging for channel and harbor projects, according to McManus' forthcoming study. Yet he describes that damage as "essentially permanent."

"You cannot grow a coral on an airstrip because they don't grow on airstrips; they grow underwater," says Edgardo D. Gomez, a marine biologist and a professor emeritus at the University of the Philippines. And because the Spratly reefs have such a high degree of species endemism, Gomez adds, "We may have lost a number of species that we never discovered."

Scientists also worry that China's island-building campaign could exacerbate the risk of a fisheries collapse in the South China Sea. Decades of commercial trawl fishing in the sea's coastal areas have already led to declining catches in most of its fisheries, and many Chinese and Southeast Asian fishing fleets—some with support from government programs—have begun to target deep-water habitats, according to the Fisheries Center at the University of British Columbia.

The Spratlys and other offshore reefs have long been somewhat protected from these pressures because fishermen saw them as difficult and dangerous to access, scientists say. But China's new islands could change the equation by providing offshore harbors for Chinese fishing fleets. Wilkinson says that once ports are established on the new islands, "fishing boats will use the area more and more until eventually they deplete populations."

In June, China's State Oceanic Administration said in a statement that environmental protection measures, including advanced dredging techniques, had been implemented during planning and construction of its artificial islands, and that the islands would eventually have facilities that deal with environmental protection. "Impact on coral reef ecology is localized, temporary, controllable, and restorable," the agency added. Two coral reef experts from China—at the Chinese University of Hong Kong and the government's South China Sea Institute of Oceanology—did not respond to interview requests for this article.

Carpenter says the South China Sea is so politically sensitive that marine biologists from Taiwan, Hong Kong, and mainland China typically do not feel comfortable discussing the ecological impacts of the island-building campaign in public. But in private, he adds, "they'll tell you they're incensed, just like we are."

Print Citations

CMS: Ives, Mike. "The Rising Environmental Toll of China's Offshore Island Grab." In *The Reference Shelf: The South China Sea Conflict*, edited by Betsy Maury, 98-102. Ipswich, MA: H.W. Wilson, 2018.

MLA: Ives, Mike. "The Rising Environmental Toll of China's Offshore Island Grab." *The Reference Shelf: The South China Sea Conflict*. Ed. Betsy Maury. Ipswich: H.W. Wilson, 2018. 98-102. Print.

APA: Ives, M. (2018). The rising environmental toll of China's offshore island grab. In Betsy Maury (Ed.), *The reference shelf: The South China Sea conflict* (pp. 98-102). Ipswich, MA: H.W. Wilson. (Original work published 2016)

One of the World's Biggest Fisheries Is on the Verge of Collapse

By Rachael Bale
National Geographic, August 29, 2016

Puerto Princesa, Philippines—One time Christopher Tubo caught a 660-pound blue marlin in the South China Sea. That was years ago, when the fishing there was good, he says. He would come home from a trip with dozens of valuable fish like tuna and a haul of other species.

"Here there's none of that," he says, looking toward the Sulu Sea, the Philippine sea where he's been fishing for the past four years. His two boats, traditional Filipino outriggers called *bancas,* float in the shallow water nearby, new coats of white paint on the decks, drying in the sun.

Tubo sits on a wooden bench in front of his home, which is perched on stilts above the bay. One of his four kids wraps an arm around his leg. Worn T-shirts and shorts flutter on clotheslines behind them.

Glancing at his wife, Leah, and the other children, he says, "It's just chance, whether or not we can feed our families now."

Tubo lives in Puerto Princesa, a city of 255,000 on Palawan, a long finger of an island that faces the Sulu Sea and the Philippine archipelago to the east and the contested South China Sea to the west. He's one of the more than 320,000 fishermen in the Philippines who have traditionally made their livelihood from the South China Sea—and one of a growing number who are now fishing in other, less ecologically rich waters. That's because about eight years ago China took a more assertive posture in the region, ramping up its intimidation of other fishermen and eventually building military installations on contested islands.

It was after a Chinese coast guard vessel attacked a friend's boat with water cannons that Tubo quit fishing the South China Sea.

"One minute you'll see an airplane, then there's a naval boat," he says. "If we keep going over there, maybe we won't be able to go home to our families."

"As they see it, it's theirs now, and Filipinos are forbidden," says Henry Tesorio, an elected councilor for a fishing village in Puerto Princesa.

Vietnamese fishermen could say the same thing. Some 200 Vietnamese from the island of Ly Son, 15 miles off the mainland, reported being attacked by Chinese boats in 2015, according to local Vietnamese government officials.

Tubo's decision is a reflection of the rising tensions in the region, which have ignited an increasingly fierce competition for natural resources, among other things. Encompassing 1.4 million square miles, the South China Sea is of critical economic, military, and environmental significance: Some $5.3 trillion in international trade plies its waters annually. It is richer in biodiversity than nearly any other marine ecosystem on the planet, and its fish provide food and jobs for millions of people in the 10 surrounding countries and territories.

Of those, seven—Brunei, China, Indonesia, Malaysia, the Philippines, Taiwan, and Vietnam—-have competing claims. If a military conflict were to break out, it could involve two world powers, China and the United States, a longtime ally of the Philippines. That's why the dispute has commanded worldwide attention.

Another serious yet less publicized threat looms: overfishing. The South China Sea is one of the world's most important fisheries, employing more than 3.7 million people and generating billions of dollars every year. But after decades of free-for-all fishing, stocks are dwindling, threatening the food security and economic growth of the rapidly developing nations that rely on them.

China asserts a right to almost the entire sea. It has demarcated a broad, U-shaped area that it says has historically been China's but that under international law includes the waters of other nations. Every other country in the South China Sea dispute, including the Philippines, bases its claims on the United Nations Convention on the Law of the Sea, the international pact that defines maritime zones and first went into effect in 1994.

Opposing Beijing's expansionist claims, in 2013 the Philippines brought a case against China before a tribunal at the Permanent Court of Arbitration, a forum for settling international disputes, in The Hague. China refused to participate. On July 12, 2016, the tribunal ruled in favor of the Philippines on almost all its claims, declaring that China had forfeited the possibility of any historically based rights when it ratified the UN convention in 1996. China vowed to ignore the tribunal's ruling.

This dispute over the South China Sea intensifies competition among fishermen, and the resulting scramble for fish inflames the dispute. Today some waters have less than one-tenth of the stocks they had six decades ago. And high-value fish such as tuna and grouper are becoming scarcer.

"What we're looking at is potentially one of the world's worst fisheries collapses ever," says John McManus, a marine ecologist at the Rosenstiel School at the University of Miami who studies reefs in the region. "We're talking hundreds and hundreds of species that will collapse, and they could collapse relatively quickly, one after another."

Fishermen on the Front Lines

When coastal waters became depleted, many fishermen were forced to venture beyond national limits and into disputed areas to make a living. Meanwhile China began bolstering its claims by aggressively supporting its fishermen. It has consolidated the coast guard, militarized fishing fleets, and promoted its subsidies for fuel and better boats. There's even a subsidy specifically for Chinese fishermen to work the waters around the contested Spratly Islands, more than 500 miles to the south of China's southernmost point (a port on the island of Hainan).

"The only reason that smaller [Chinese] fishermen go out to the Spratlys is because they're paid to do so," says Gregory Poling, the director of the Asia Maritime Transparency Initiative, at the Washington, D.C.-based think tank, the Center for Strategic and International Studies. This extra pressure has sped up the depletion of fish stocks, he says.

The Chinese also are building artificial islands atop reefs in the Spratlys to support military installations there. "Possession is nine-tenths of the law," says Zachary Abuza, an expert on Southeast Asian politics and maritime security at the National War College, in Washington, D.C. "China is trying to enforce its sovereignty through the construction of these islands and by denying other countries access to natural resources."

Eugenio Bito-onon, Jr., is a former mayor of the Kalayaan municipality that includes islands in the Spratlys. An outspoken advocate for the Philippines' claims, he has seen firsthand how China uses its fishermen to strengthen its claim to the region. I met Bito-onon in the municipality's cramped satellite office in Puerto Princesa, where the wall of one room displays a gigantic map of the South China Sea marked up with his own handwritten labels and colored dots showing which countries claim which features.

He pulled up Google Earth on his laptop and found Thitu Island, in the Spratlys known locally as Pagasa, where some 200 Filipinos, including a small number of troops, live part-time, their presence demonstrating his country's claim to the island. ice, clothing, soap, and other necessities must be brought in by boat or airlift, and two government-owned generators are the only source of electricity. Bito-onon pointed out just how close Chinese-claimed Subi Reef is to Thitu. So close, he said, that on a clear day residents can see it on the horizon.

After decades of free-for-all fishing, stocks are dwindling, threatening the food security and economic growth of the rapidly developing nations that rely on them.

Even closer are Chinese fishing boats that he says have fished the reefs empty. "For the past three years, [the Chinese] never leave," Bito-onon said from behind his laptop, now displaying satellite imagery of reefs around Thitu. "Chinese fishing boats come and go, replacing each other," he says, but there are never not boats within sight of the island.

Gilbert Elefane, the Filipino captain of a tuna boat based in the municipality of Quezon, on Palawan, says he now sees up to a hundred boats, many Chinese, on a single two-week fishing trip in the South China Sea. Just a few years ago, he says he'd have seen no more than 30.

Beijing has provided military training and sophisticated GPS and communications technology to its fishermen so they can call in the coast guard if they have a run-in with a foreign law enforcement vessel or alert the coast guard of the presence of fishermen from other countries.

In the face of China's island building, Vietnam has done some small-scale land reclamation of its own in an attempt to bolster its capacity in the Spratlys. Its efforts, however, have been less destructive than China's.

Lawless Sea

As long as the conflict in the South China Sea continues, it will be nearly impossible to regulate fishing.

When one country tries to protect its fishing grounds, tensions flare. In March, for instance, Indonesian maritime law enforcement officials arrested eight Chinese on charges of illegal fishing. The fishermen were less than three miles from Indonesia's Natuna Islands. The Natunas themselves are not in dispute, but the waters north of them, which are particularly rich in gas, have become a new flashpoint. Under international law they're Indonesian, but they partially overlap with China's U-shaped line claims, so China says it has a right to fish there.

When Indonesia's vessel began towing the Chinese boat back to port, an armed Chinese coast guard ship appeared and began ramming the Chinese boat to break it free. The Indonesians were forced to let the boat go and retreat.

"It's unclear whose laws you're enforcing when you have seven overlapping sets of fisheries laws," Poling says. "States have a vested interest in purposely violating fishing laws of other states."

That's because abiding by another country's fishing law amounts to accepting that nation's jurisdiction over the region, which no country has been willing to do.

In 2012 a Philippine Navy warship tried to arrest Chinese fishermen at Scarborough Shoal, about 138 miles from the Philippine coast, on suspicion of illegal fishing and poaching rare corals, giant clams, and sharks. A Chinese coast guard ship intervened to prevent the arrests, forcing a standoff. Ten weeks later both sides agreed to withdraw, but after the Philippine warship left, China's ship remained, effectively seizing control of the shoal.

As Filipino fishermen have seen their catches—and the fish themselves—getting smaller, they've increasingly been resorting to dangerous, illegal fishing methods. Blast fishing, which Filipinos call "bong bong" fishing, involves setting off homemade bombs underwater to kill dozens of fish at one time. Cyanide fishing, which involves squirting fish in the face with poison to stun them, is used to catch live reef fish to supply high-end live seafood restaurants in Hong Kong and other large Asian cities. Both practices kill coral and other fish, collateral damage that's pushing the sea closer to an overfishing crisis.

Reefs under Siege

More destructive to the reefs, however, are China's island building and giant clam poaching, which account for most of the documented reef destruction in the South China Sea, an area totaling 62 square miles. Island building grinds up corals for use as foundation material, smothers reefs that become the base of islands, and creates sediment plumes that suffocate nearby reefs. Dredging to deepen ports also causes serious damage. And poaching of giant clams entails digging up entire areas of reef to get to the shells.

When a reef is destroyed, the ecosystem unravels. Reef fish lose their habitat, and pelagic fish such as tuna lose an important source of food. Furthermore, reefs in the South China Sea are connected. Fish larvae from one reef ride the current across the sea to repopulate another reef. If a reef disappears, so does that source of larvae, increasing the chance that local extirpations of fish species will be permanent.

"It's quite possible we're seeing a serious decline in about half of the reefs," McManus, the marine ecologist, says. "That's what I expect will happen, if it hasn't happened already. It's just total destruction."

McManus says that many of the damaged reefs will be able to recover in a decade or two—if the island building and destructive giant clam poaching stop. He champions the idea of a "peace park," a kind of marine protected area where all countries would put a freeze on their claims and halt all activities, like island building, that bolster those claims.

Experts also say cooperative regional management could go a long way toward making the South China Sea fishery sustainable. It would require dramatic cutbacks in the number of fishing boats and restrictions on fishing methods such as the use of huge fishing vessels that use powerful lights at night to attract tuna. All this would in turn mean helping fishermen find other ways to earn a living.

Under a sustainable management plan, tuna and mackerel could recover 17-fold by 2045, Rashid Sumaila and William Cheung at the University of British Columbia predicted in a 2015 report. Reef fish would recover up to 15 percent, and the catch and value of reef fish would also increase. Sharks and groupers, which are also high-value fish, would make a comeback too.

But Poling, of the Center for Strategic and International Studies, questions whether such a plan could be devised in time to prevent the fishery from collapsing.

"What that requires is setting aside the disputes," he says. "It's possible—it's just not likely. In order to have a successful joint management system, the first step is to agree on what area you're talking about." If China clings to its expanded jurisdictional claim while other countries base their claims on international law, agreement won't be possible, he says.

As it now stands, the South China Sea's most important resource—its fish—is disappearing, and countries are either passively standing by or actively encouraging their fishermen to take more.

Print Citations

CMS: Bale, Rachael. "One of the Biggest Fisheries Is on the Verge of Collapse." In *The Reference Shelf: The South China Sea Conflict*, edited by Betsy Maury, 103-108. Ipswich, MA: H.W. Wilson, 2018.

MLA: Bale, Rachael. "One of the Biggest Fisheries Is on the Verge of Collapse." *The Reference Shelf: The South China Sea Conflict*. Ed. Betsy Maury. Ipswich: H.W. Wilson, 2018. 103-108. Print.

APA: Bale, R. (2018). One of the biggest fisheries is on the verge of collapse. In Betsy Maury (Ed.), *The reference shelf: The South China Sea conflict* (pp. 103-108). Ipswich, MA: H.W. Wilson. (Original work published 2016)

A Blueprint for Fisheries Management and Environmental Cooperation in the South China Sea

Center for Strategic & International Studies, **September 13, 2017**

The South China Sea is one of the world's top five most productive fishing zones, accounting for about 12 percent of global fish catch in 2015. More than half of the fishing vessels in the world operate in these waters, employing around 3.7 million people, and likely many more engaged in illegal, unregulated, and unreported fishing. But this vital marine ecosystem is seriously threatened by overfishing encouraged by government subsidies, harmful fishing practices, and, in recent years, large-scale clam harvesting and dredging for island construction.

Total fish stocks in the South China Sea have been depleted by 70–95 percent since the 1950s, and catch rates have declined by 66–75 percent over the last 20 years. Giant clam harvesting, dredging, and artificial island building in recent years severely damaged or destroyed over 160 square kilometers, or about 40,000 acres, of coral reefs, which were already declining by 16 percent per decade. The entire South China Sea fishery, which officially employs around 3.7 million people and helps feed hundreds of millions, is now in danger of collapse unless claimants act urgently to arrest the decline.

Article 123 of the United Nations Convention on the Law of the Sea (UNCLOS) mandates that states bordering semi-enclosed seas like the South China Sea are obligated to cooperate in areas that include the protection of the marine environment and management of fish stocks. This is reflective of the deeply interconnected ecologies of semi-enclosed seas, in which currents cycle marine life (and pollution) through the region without regard for national jurisdiction. Moreover, Article 192 of UNCLOS provides a general obligation for states to "protect and preserve the marine environment." Unlike hydrocarbons, for which exploitation rights are based only upon a state's entitlement to the continental shelf, the obligation to jointly steward living marine resources makes fisheries management and environmental protection "low hanging fruit" for cooperation in the South China Sea.

An effective system to manage South China Seas fisheries and the environment cannot be based primarily on the overlapping territorial and maritime claims, to which the fish pay no attention. Instead it must be built around the entire marine ecosystem, particularly the reef systems, on which much marine life depends. With political will, it is entirely possible for nations bordering the South China Sea to cooperatively protect these ecosystems and manage fish stocks without prejudice to their overlapping territorial and maritime claims. For instance, the Philippines, whose government is under a strict constitutional requirement to defend the nation's sovereign rights over its waters and continental shelf, could agree to cooperate on fisheries management in disputed waters under Article 123 of UNCLOS without prejudicing its claims or bestowing legitimacy on the claims of others and, therefore, without running afoul of its domestic law.

The international legal obligation to cooperate on fisheries management and the environment is matched by practical necessity. Communities all around the South China Sea are highly dependent on fish stocks for both food security and local livelihoods. Yet the region has seen catch rates plummet in recent years thanks to a combination of overfishing and willful environmental destruction. In the South China Sea, fish

> **Total fish stocks in the South China Sea have been depleted by 70-95 percent since the 1950s, and catch rates have declined by 66-75 percent of the last 20 years.**

may spawn in one nation's exclusive economic zone (EEZ), live as juveniles in another's, and spend most of their adult lives in a third. Overfishing or environmental destruction at any point in the chain affects all those who live around the sea. The entire South China Sea is teetering on the edge of a fisheries collapse, and the only way to avoid it is through multilateral cooperation in disputed waters.

To that end, claimants should agree to:

1. Establish a Fishery and Environmental Management Area in the South China Sea with implementation and enforcement drawing from successful precedents, including the Great Barrier Reef Marine Park and the Convention for the Protection of the Marine Environment of the North-East Atlantic (OSPAR Convention). This would constitute a series of distinct ecosystem-based fisheries zones covering the reefs that are vital to regional fish stocks, including the Paracel Islands, Spratly Islands, Scarborough Shoal, and Luconia Shoals, as well as the waters between, in which pelagic species are fished.

    *   This management area would not necessitate a complete ban on fishing. Instead it would consist of a patchwork of tailored fisheries zones. Some of these would be no-catch zones to allow dangerously depleted fisheries to replenish, but in others only certain types of fishing would be restricted, while still others might involve no restrictions at all. See the map below for an example of this type of scheme as applied to the Great Barrier Reef.

    *   Claimants should publicly agree that involvement in the establishment and enforcement of the management area would be without prejudice to their existing territorial and maritime claims and could not be construed as recognition of the claims of others.

- Determinations of what types of fishing should be banned or allowed in each area should be made based solely on scientific criteria, such as reef health and importance to migratory fish stocks.

- A multilateral body should be established involving independent experts and officials from relevant fisheries, maritime, and scientific agencies from regional governments to establish the layout of the management area and make regular adjustments.

- All claimants bordering the South China Sea should be involved in the creation and management of the fisheries zones, regardless of the location of their territorial and maritime claims, because all are equally reliant upon a healthy marine ecosystem in this semi-enclosed sea. This means that Brunei, China, Indonesia, Malaysia, the Philippines, Singapore, Taiwan, and Vietnam should all be involved in the scientific research in and mapping of fisheries zones.

- An advisory body on the management of pelagic fish species should be established to include both the South China Sea claimants and Gulf of Thailand littoral countries. The latter need not be involved in the creation of fisheries zones covering reef fish in the South China Sea, but should be consulted regarding zones aimed at managing migratory stocks that travel between the two bodies of water.

2. Split enforcement responsibilities between occupiers and flag states.
    - Claimants should bear responsibility for monitoring and interdiction of ships violating the mutually agreed-upon fishing restrictions within 12 nautical miles of outposts they occupy on disputed features AND in areas of the management area within 200 nautical miles of their coastlines. In areas of overlapping jurisdiction, the 12-mile zone around occupied features should take precedence. If two such zones overlap, a median line should be used to separate the two areas of responsibility. These enforcement zones are illustrated in the interactive map below and in the static graphics at the end of this blueprint.

    - These jurisdictional zones would not constitute a judgment about sovereignty over occupied features or their legal status (as islands, rocks, low-tide elevations, or submerged features). They also would not prejudice any future delimitation of maritime boundaries.

    - Patrol and interdiction of ships violating the mutually agreed-upon fishing restrictions in all other parts of the management area may be undertaken by any claimant. This includes all waters and unoccupied features farther than 200 nautical miles from coastlines. Claimants should seek to coordinate patrols, including with the eventual use of ship-rider agreements, and share maritime domain awareness information in these areas.

- Prosecution of ships from a claimant nation that violate fishing restrictions in the management area should be the responsibility of the flag state. The arresting party should arrange to transfer such vessels and their crew in a timely manner. Prosecution of violators from non-claimant countries should be the responsibility of the arresting party.

3. Agree not to use subsidies to encourage fishing within the already overfished South China Sea.
   - All claimants should agree to forego geographically defined subsidies that might encourage fishing within the management area.

   - Claimants should agree that fishermen found to violate the management area's restrictions would lose access to any existing government subsidy and support programs meant to support the fishing industry.

4. Coordinate efforts to reintroduce giant clams and other threatened species such as sea turtles to depopulated reefs in the South China Sea.
   - This effort should be led by a consortium of universities and research organizations, such as those in China and Southeast Asia already engaged in raising giant clams in captivity, with governments providing funding, coordination, and logistical support.

   - Each claimant should be responsible for planting clams and reintroducing other species on reefs it currently occupies. Eventually, unoccupied reefs should be repopulated by multinational civilian teams, though in the short and medium term, priority should be given to reefs near occupied features as they will be much easier to protect from poachers. All claimants should agree that such activities would be undertaken without regard to or prejudice for territorial claims.

5. Avoid activities that damage the marine environment or alter the seabed.
   - Claimants should refrain from any intentional destruction of marine habitats, including by dredging, land reclamation, or construction of facilities on unoccupied reefs.

   - Claimants should commit to perform and publicly release environmental impact assessments before undertaking construction or renovation work on their occupied features.

6. Cooperate on marine scientific research, which is necessary to assess the health of the maritime environment and effectively implement conservation efforts.
   - Claimants should coordinate joint marine scientific research cruises

throughout the South China Sea with experts from all claimants invited to participate.

- Each claimant should facilitate visits by experts from other claimant nations to conduct research on islands and reefs that it occupies, with due regard given to the need to restrict access to sensitive military sites. Claimants should all agree that research trips would be organized without prejudice to the outstanding claims of other parties and that participation would not imply recognition on the part of individual researchers or governments of the claims of the organizer.

- Claimants should host regular scientific workshops supported by all neighboring governments with participation of experts from across the region and beyond.

- Governments should invest, both individually and as a group, in programs to raise public awareness of the importance of and threats to fisheries as a common, renewable resource.

Print Citations

CMS: "A Blueprint for Fisheries Management and Environmental Cooperation in the South China Sea." In *The Reference Shelf: The South China Sea Conflict,* edited by Betsy Maury, 109-113. Ipswich, MA: H.W. Wilson, 2018.

MLA: "A Blueprint for Fisheries Management and Environmental Cooperation in the South China Sea." *The Reference Shelf: The South China Sea Conflict.* Ed. Betsy Maury. Ipswich: H.W. Wilson, 2018. 109-113. Print.

APA: Center for Strategic & International Studies. (2018). A blueprint for fisheries management and environmental cooperation in the South China Sea. In Betsy Maury (Ed.), *The reference shelf: The South China Sea conflict* (pp. 109-113). Ipswich, MA: H.W. Wilson. (Original work published 2017)

Japan and China Successfully Extract 'Combustible Ice' from Seafloor in Potential Energy Breakthrough

By Matthew Brown

The Associated Press via *The Independent*, May 19, 2017

Commercial development of the globe's huge reserves of a frozen fossil fuel known as "combustible ice" has moved closer to reality after Japan and China successfully extracted the material from the seafloor off their coastlines.

But experts said Friday that large-scale production remains many years away — and if not done properly could flood the atmosphere with climate-changing greenhouse gases.

Combustible ice is a frozen mixture of water and concentrated natural gas. Technically known as methane hydrate, it can be lit on fire in its frozen state and is believed to comprise one of the world's most abundant fossil fuels.

The official Chinese news agency Xinhua reported that the fuel was successfully mined by a drilling rig operating in the South China Sea on Thursday. Chinese Minister of Land and Resources Jiang Daming declared the event a breakthrough moment heralding a potential "global energy revolution."

A drilling crew in Japan reported a similar successful operation two weeks earlier, on 4 May offshore the Shima Peninsula.

For Japan, methane hydrate offers the chance to reduce its heavy reliance of imported fuels if it can tap into reserves off its coastline. In China, it could serve as a cleaner substitute for coal-burning power plants and steel factories that have polluted much of the country with lung-damaging smog.

The South China Sea has become a focal point of regional political tensions as China has claimed huge swaths of disputed territory as its own. Previous sea oil exploration efforts by China met resistance, especially from Vietnam, but its methane hydrate operation was described as being outside the most hotly contested areas.

Methane hydrate has been found beneath seafloors and buried inside Arctic permafrost and beneath Antarctic ice. The United States and India also have research programme pursuing technologies to capture the fuel.

Estimates of worldwide reserves range from 280 trillion cubic metres (10,000 trillion cubic feet) up to 2,800 trillion cubic metres (100,000 trillion cubic feet), according to the US Energy Information Administration. By comparison, total worldwide production of natural gas was 3.5 billion cubic metres (124 billion cubic feet) in 2015, the most recent year available.

That means methane hydrate reserves could meet global gas demands for 80 to 800 years at current consumption rates.

Yet efforts to successfully extract the fuel at a profit have eluded private and state-owned energy companies for decades. That's in part because of the high cost of extraction techniques, which can use large amounts of water or carbon dioxide to flood methane hydrate reserves so the fuel can be released and brought to the surface.

Japan first extracted some of the material in 2013 but ended the effort due to sand from the seafloor clogging machinery, according to the country's Ministry of Economy Trade and Tourism.

There are also environmental concerns.

If methane hydrate leaks during the extraction process, it can increase greenhouse gas emissions. The fuel also could displace renewables such as solar and wind power, said David Sandalow, a former senior official with the US State Department now at Columbia University's Center on Global Energy Policy.

However, if it can be used without leaking, it has the potential to replace dirtier coal in the power sector.

> **Methane hydrate can be lit on fire in its frozen state and would represent a major new fossil fuel reserve if it could be commercially developed.**

"The climate implications of producing natural gas hydrates are complicated. There are potential benefits, but substantial risks," Sandalow said.

Commercial-scale production could be "transformative for northeast Asia, particularly for Japan, which imports nearly all its hydrocarbon needs," said James Taverner, a senior energy industry researcher at IHS Market, a London-based consulting firm.

The consensus within the industry is that commercial development won't happen until at least 2030. Smaller scale output could happen as early as 2020, said Tim Collett, a scientist with the US Geological Survey.

"The path to understanding when or if gas hydrates will be commercially produced will need many similar and more extended testing efforts," Collett said.

Print Citations

CMS: Brown, Matthew. "Japan and China Successfully Extract 'Combustible Ice' from Seafloor in Potential Energy Breakthrough." In *The Reference Shelf: The South China Sea Conflict*, edited by Betsy Maury, 114-116. Ipswich, MA: H.W. Wilson, 2018.

MLA: Brown, Matthew. "Japan and China Successfully Extract 'Combustible Ice' from Seafloor in Potential Energy Breakthrough." *The Reference Shelf: The South China Sea Conflict*. Ed. Betsy Maury. Ipswich: H.W. Wilson, 2018. 114-116. Print.

APA: Brown, M. (2018). Japan and China Successfully Extract 'Combustible Ice' from Seafloor in Potential Energy Breakthrough. In Betsy Maury (Ed.), *The reference shelf: The South China Sea conflict* (pp. 114-116). Ipswich, MA: H.W. Wilson. (Original work published 2017)

5

Diplomacy, Deterrence and Freedom of Navigation

Philippine and US marine officials, led by US marine Brigadier General Paul Kennedy (4th L) and Philippine Major General Alexander Labutan (2nd R), pose for photos during the opening ceremony of the annual Philippine-US naval exercise (PHIBLEX) in Manila on October 1, 2015. US Pacific commanders held talks with the Philippine military on ways to strengthen US capacity in the region to deter conflict and maintain freedom of navigation in the south China sea, a Filipino spokesman said.

International Waters: FONOPS and the Open Ocean

One of the goals for the United States, Japan, and other international nations peripherally involved in the South China Sea conflict is to defend the principles of the United Nations Convention on the Law of the Sea (UNCLOS) regarding fair use of the seas as a shared resource for all humanity. Towards this end, the United States has encouraged negotiation within the United Nations, and has engaged in naval exercises in the disputed area, disputing China's claims while asserting the US right to peacefully pass through the sea. Within the United States, there have been many suggestions for how to modify China policy moving forward, with some stressing diplomacy, while others favor direct intervention and military force, and others favor a blend of techniques to deter further escalation.

Freedom of Navigation

The United States never ratified the UNCLOS and thus is not legally bound to adhere to the treaty. However, since the late 1980s, the United States has used military ships to challenge territorial claims over important international nautical routes, citing what the United States calls "Freedom of Navigation" or "FON," defined as the freedom to navigate freely through all international waters.

The freedom for sovereign ships to navigate open waters has long been a subject of intense interest for governments, military leaders, and commercial traders. Scholarly studies of the "Rhodian Sea Law," documents from the seventh or eighth century CE, indicate that the empire of ancient Rome struggled to develop international conventions for the use of the oceans, but it is unclear whether a legitimate body of law emerged from these efforts.[1] The first widespread treatise on maritime law was the *Consulat de Mar*, or Consulate of the Sea, a collection of maritime ordinances and customs compiled in Catalan in the 1200s for use by judges with authority over maritime commerce. The documents contain 294 separate legal principles and detailing the function of maritime courts.[2] The book was translated into English and became the basis for British maritime law and thus was also the inspiration for nautical law within the United States.

One of the central facets of international maritime law has been to preserve use of the ocean as a human right and shared resource, and not simply a territorial privilege for those living nearest to a body of water or controlling features that lie within the world's seas, straits, and oceans. Each version of UNCLOS has preserved this ancient idea about the ownership of the seas, holding that no nation can exert any ownership over the ocean and can assert only limited rights to the waters nearest the nation's territorial properties. The United States' commitment to freedom of navigation is partially based on military goals—preserving the ability to dispatch ships to address military conflicts that occur anywhere in the world—and partially based on the desire to preserve shipping routes for commercial traffic. The most recent version of UNCLOS preserved this right by designating all waters more than 200 nautical miles from the furthest legitimately owned territory as international waters, or "the high seas," which are collectively owned by all of humanity. In addition, all 119 nations that ratified the 1982 UNCLOS agreed to allow "innocent passage" of ships anywhere in the ocean, even within a nation's 12-nautical mile territorial sea.

The United States never fully accepted the responsibilities of UNCLOS, but the Reagan administration worked to establish a national maritime strategy, known as the US Oceans Policy of 1983, that mirrored the UN treaty. Towards this end, the U.S. Navy was empowered to conduct Freedom of Navigation Operations (FONOPS) to preserve United States and international access to the seas. These include military operations with the express purpose of challenging "...excessive maritime claims" and diplomatic efforts to resolve territorial issues with regard to international passages.[3] The United States conducted dozens of FONOPS in different parts of the world from the 1980s to 2017. Though FONOPS in the South China Sea have been covered widely in the media, the United States engages in similar operations around the world. In 2016, for instance, the United States also engaged in FONOPS to challenge territorial claims made by Brazil, Venezuela, Italy, Malta, India, Iran, Oman, Japan, Vietnam, and Indonesia.

Within the South China Sea, US FONOPS began, in earnest, on October 27, 2015, when the USS *Lassen* conducted a controversial FONOPS near the Spratly Islands, claiming innocent passage to travel 12 nautical miles from Subi Reef, without prior notification to Chinese authorities. China criticized the operation as unnecessarily provocative and warned that the nation would not be threatened into abandoning its claims to occupied islands and reefs.

Then, in January of 2016, the USS *Curtis Wilbur* passed within 12 nautical miles of Triton Island on the Paracel Island Chain, with China calling the operation "unprofessional and irresponsible." FONOPS continued with a May 10, 2016 passage within near the Fiery Cross Reef in the Spratly Chain, then an October 2016, FONOPS near the Paracel Islands, during which three Chinese military ships following the USS *Decatur* as it passed through the area. The rhetorical conflict between the two nations came to a head in December of 2016, Chinese naval forces seized a US underwater drone launched by an unarmed survey vessel in the South China Sea. The seizure took place 50 nautical miles from Subic Bay in the Philippines, right outside China's nine-dash line, and the US government immediately protested and called the seizure unlawful. The Chinese government returned the drone, and released a statement claiming to have returned the device "After friendly consultations between China and the United States..."[4]

In 2017, the United States conducted additional FONOPS, one in May, when the USS *Dewey* passed by Mischief Reef, and another in July, when the USS *Stethem* passed by Triton Island in the Paracel archipelago,[5] then another in August, when the USS *John S. McCain* passed close to Mischief Reef, drawing criticism and claims of "provocation" from China.[6] At the same time the US was conducting FONOPS, Trump was reportedly courting negotiations with China to deal with nuclear proliferation in North Korea. Despite this, FONOPS continued into the fall, with another exercise reported on October 10, 2017, when a guided-missile destroyer, the USS *Chaffee*, carried out maneuvering operations near the Paracel Islands, but not crossing into China's claimed "territorial sea."[7]

Opinions on the effectiveness and strategic merit of FONOPS vary widely. Many military analysts have encouraged the practice and opined that the United States needs to invite other nations to participate, signifying, to China, a broader international objection to their military buildup. Others disagree, arguing that FONOPS accomplish little and create additional tension where negotiation could otherwise occur. For instance, writing in *The Diplomat*, scholar Mark Valencia, from the National Institute for South China Sea Studies, argues that what he calls "gunboat diplomacy" might not be necessary to assert the US position and that the United States might, as many other nations have, simply signal its position through political communications with China, rather than relying on a symbolic show of force. Valencia argues further that, because China has not tried to use the Spratly Islands to create a new "baseline" for the measurement of their territorial sea, the United States is essentially challenging *potential* claims that have not yet been made. Valencia thus argues, as other analysts have, that US policy in the region is ineffective and that the United States should shift to viewing the conflict as a chance for negotiation and compromise.[8]

Deterrence and Diplomacy

An underlying truth in the South China Sea controversy is that neither China nor the United States are likely going to take action that would lead to direct military conflict. This is partially because, as two of the world's major powers, such a conflict would be globally disastrous and would result in substantial loss of power and economic influence for both nations. Furthermore, China and the United States are economically codependent on one another and the loss of the trade agreements between the two nations would likewise be devastating to their shared economic interests. The legitimate danger in the South China Sea conflict is therefore the creation of a "proxy" war, with either the United States or China, or *both*, supporting a conflict through a proxy nation or group, such as occurred in the Vietnam and Korean conflicts.[9]

Some analysts believe that the United States could end the conflict by taking a more aggressive military stance. For instance, specialist Alexander Vuving, writing in *Foreign Policy* magazine, argued in February of 2017 that the United States and its allies should essentially mirror China's activities in the sea, building rings of civilian, law enforcement, and military vessels around islands and other rocks and so essentially blocking access to Chinese development.[10] Essentially, Vuving's solution is one of deterrence, with the United States upping its presence, and thus (hopefully) deterring further buildup from China. There is, however, no guarantee that such a strategy would be effective and the risks involved have led some critics to argue that further military escalation is irresponsible.

Writing in the *Straits Times*, Professor Joseph Chinyong, of the S. Rajaratnam School of International Studies, argues that the United States had not been committed to securing peace in southeast Asia. Chinyong cites the $425 million spent over five years towards the nation's Maritime Security Initiative, compared to more than $10 billion a year on Afghanistan operations as evidence of the nation's limited investment. Chinyong thus proposes a five-pillar approach to a possible US strategy, based on (as the first pillar) adherence to international law, meaning that the United States should ratify UNCLOS and make a commitment to other UN conventions, like the International Court of Justice to signify the nation's commitment to international law and negotiation overall. Second, Chinyong supports continued FONOPS, especially with international involvement, but argues that such operations will be ineffective unless conducted within a broader diplomatic framework. The final three pillars proposed by Chinyong include creating incentives (in the form of new trade agreements) that provide benefits to China in return for reducing military buildup, engaging in aggressive diplomatic engagement accompanying all other activities, and finally, relying on the Association of Southeast Asian Nations (ASEAN) states organization as a partner in attempting to address the issue.[11]

US policy between 2015 and 2017 achieved little and arguably eroded the relationship between the United States and China. Moving forward, analysts across the spectrum agree that a new strategy is needed, though there is far less agreement regarding the form that this new strategy should take. Unless the United States demonstrates a stronger commitment to international law overall, and deepens cooperative efforts to address international disputes, the situation may continue largely unchanged for the foreseeable future. If the United States chooses a more direct, military route, relations with China will likely deteriorate and, while open warfare between the two nations is unlikely, violence may intensify, with US allies in the region standing to lose the most from the escalation.

Micah L. Issitt

Works Used

Benedict, Robert D. "The Historical Position of the Rhodian Law." *Yale Law Journal*. Vol. 18, No. 4. 1909, 223-42.

Chinyong, Joseph. "Five Pillars for a US Strategy on the South China Sea." *The Straits Times*. Singapore Press Holdings Ltd. Co. Aug 1 2017. Web. 18 Dec 2017.

Jiang, Steven and Kevin Bohn. "China Returns Seized US Underwater Drone." *CNN*. CNN Politics. Dec 20 2016. Web. 19 Dec 2017.

LaGrone, Sam. "Chine Chides U.S. over Latest South China Sea Freedom of Navigation Operation." *USNI*. U.S. Naval Institute. Oct 11 2017. Web. 18 Dec 2017.

Pesek, William. "Making Sense of the South China Sea Dispute." *Forbes*. Forbes Inc. Aug 22 2017. Web. 18 Dec 2017.

Smith, Robert S. "Recent Criticism of the Consulate of the Sea." *The Hispanic American Historical Review*. Vol. 14, No. 3 (Aug 1934), 359-63.

Standifer, Cid. "UPDATED: A Brief History of U.S. Freedom of Navigation Operations in the South China Sea." *USNI*. US Naval Institute. Jul 2 2017. Web. 18 Dec 2017.

Sterling, Joe. "US Destroyer in South China Sea Called 'Provocation' by Beijing." *CNN*. CNN Politics. Aug 10 2017. Web. 18 Dec 2017.

"U.S. Department of Defense Freedom of Navigation Program." *DOD*. Department of Defense. Mar 2015. Web. 18 Dec 2017.

Valencia, Mark J. "Are US FONOPs in the South China Sea Necessary?" *The Diplomat*. The Diplomat. Oct 28 2017. Web. 18 Dec 2017.

Vuving, Alexander L. "How America Can Take Control in the South China Sea." *Foreign Policy*. Foreign Policy Institute, Inc. Feb 13 2017. Web. 18 Dec 2017.

Notes

1. Benedict, "The Historical Position of the Rhodian Law."
2. Smith, "Recent Criticism of the Consulate of the Sea."
3. "U.S. Department of Defense Freedom of Navigation Program," *DOD*.
4. Jiang and Bohn, "China Returns Seized US Underwater Drone."
5. Standifer, "UPDATED: A Brief History of U.S. Freedom of Navigation Operations in the South China Sea."
6. Sterling, "US Destroyer in South China Sea Called 'Provocation' by Beijing."
7. LaGrone, "China Chides U.S. over Latest South China Sea Freedom of Navigation Operation."
8. Valencia, "Are US FONOPs in the South China Sea Necessary?"
9. Pesek, "Making Sense of the South China Sea Dispute."
10. Vuving, "How American Can Take Control in the South China Sea."
11. Chinyong, "Five Pillars for a US Strategy on the South China Sea."

The U.S. FON Program in the South China Sea

By Lynn Kuok
Brookings, June 7, 2016

U.S. freedom of navigation (FON) operations have recently come under scrutiny with assertions near contested features in the South China Sea. While some question whether they are necessary, there are strong legal and practical imperatives supporting their conduct. FON operations help to ensure that the hard-earned compromises reached during the Third United Nations Conference on the Law of the Sea (1973-1982) are maintained both by word and deed. The Vienna Convention on the Law of Treaties states that "subsequent practice" shall be taken into account in interpreting treaties. If the United States fails to consistently assert is maritime rights under international law, these might be lost over time. Moreover, as a practical matter, rights not used are of little real value.

FON operations are part of the broader U.S. FON Program, which proceeds on a triple track. Criticism that the United States is prioritizing physical assertions over diplomatic and multilateral efforts is unwarranted. An examination of U.S. responses to three types of excessive maritime claims that are particularly problematic in the region—the insistence on prior authorization or notification for warships to exercise innocent passage, the prohibition of military activities in the EEZ, and the drawing of straight baselines when geographic conditions for doing so are not satisfied—demonstrates that the United States has been meticulous in diplomatically protesting excessive maritime claims and in setting out its (and the majority) interpretation of international law. FON operations assert rights available to all user states and cannot validly be described as a "use of force" or even

> **Effectively employed, FON operations could help counter China's attempts to assert de facto control over the South China Sea.**

"militarization". Rather, such assertions are legitimate exercises of rights vested under international law.

In the South China Sea, FON operations have taken on additional significance given China's strategic ambiguity. In the past, FON operations were undertaken to challenge excessive maritime claims. They are now, however, arguably being conducted to *pre-empt* them—a course of action necessitated by China's continued refusal to clarify its claims. Such operations may, accordingly, be better framed as *assertions of maritime rights* (so that these rights are reinforced and not detracted from in the future), rather than as challenges to excessive maritime claims. This recasting is particularly appropriate in the Spratlys where China has been especially vague about its maritime claims.

Effectively employed, FON operations could help counter China's attempts to assert de facto control over the South China Sea. They will also raise the costs of Beijing declaring straight baselines around the Spratlys and attempting to convert the waters within these lines to internal waters.

The widely anticipated tribunal decision in the Philippines case against China will facilitate the planning, execution and messaging of FON operations by clarifying the status of features. Insofar as the conduct of FON operations is consistent with the tribunal's award, it will bolster the United States' ability to argue that its actions are in accordance with international law. Regular assertions of maritime rights in respect of features that are the subject of the tribunal's decision will give the award teeth and render it more difficult for China to ignore the ruling.

The South China Sea dispute is about much more than mere "rocks". It concerns maritime rights and the preservation of the system of international law. More broadly, how the United States and China interact in the South China Sea has important implications for their relationship elsewhere and on other issues.

This paper recommends that the United States consider the following:

1. Continue to regularly assert maritime rights in the South China Sea, including in the Spratlys
2. Clearly put on record the maritime right the United States is asserting at the time of a FON operation
3. Publish a consolidated list of all diplomatic protests made in respect of excessive maritime claims
4. Quietly persuade other states to conduct FON operations, engage in joint patrols and/or issue diplomatic protests
5. Clarify that the U.S.-China MOU regarding rules of behavior for safety of air and maritime encounters applies to FON operations, and extend the agreement to apply to coastguard
6. Redouble diplomatic efforts to arrive at a common understanding with China of what constitutes excessive maritime claims

Print Citations

CMS: Kuok, Lynn. "The U.S. FON Program in the South China Sea." In *The Reference Shelf: The South China Sea Conflict*, edited by Betsy Maury, 125-127. Ipswich, MA: H.W. Wilson, 2018.

MLA: Kuok, Lynn. "The U.S. FON Program in the South China Sea." *The Reference Shelf: The South China Sea Conflict*. Ed. Betsy Maury. Ipswich: H.W. Wilson, 2018. 125-127. Print.

APA: Kuok, L. (2018). The U.S. FON program in the South China Sea. In Betsy Maury (Ed.), *The reference shelf: The South China Sea conflict* (pp. 125-127). Ipswich, MA: H.W. Wilson. (Original work published 2016)

Freedom of Navigation Operations in the South China Sea Aren't Enough

By Julian G. Ku, M. Taylor Fravel, and Malcolm Cook
Foreign Policy, May 16, 2016

Julian G. Ku, Professor of Law, Hofstra University:
Like the two other recent U.S. freedom of navigation operations (FONOP) in the South China Sea, the most recent U.S. FONOP was designed to avoid any conflict with China's sovereignty claims. Instead, by conducting the operations under the rules of "innocent passage," the U.S. Navy assumed China might have sovereign rights, but simply challenged China's domestic law requirement that foreign warships give prior notification before entering what China claims is its territorial sea.

Despite this very limited challenge, China's reaction to the U.S. FONOP has also been largely the same. Fighter jets were scrambled, and naval assets were deployed to shadow the U.S. ship during its passage. But two new aspects to China's rhetorical response are worth noting. The shift in China's rhetoric also reveals the limits of the U.S. reliance on FONOPs as a tool to deter Chinese expansionism in the region.

First, the Chinese defense ministry has begun to suggest that the continuation of U.S. FONOPs justifies its construction of "defensive facilities" in the South China Sea. Since the most recent round of U.S. FONOPs in the region began in October 2015 (after a four-year hiatus) and the Chinese land reclamation has been going on for almost two full years, this post-hoc justification for Chinese militarization of the region is hard to swallow.

Second, the Chinese foreign ministry has started directly engaging with the narrower U.S. legal argument against a prior notification requirement for warships. In fact, it tried to isolate the U.S. legal position. Drawing a distinction between commercial and military vessels, the Chinese foreign ministry spokesman stated that "no country, except the United States believes in military vessels sailing wherever they want, which is against international law." The spokesman went on to say the U.N. Convention on the Law of the Sea (UNCLOS) "allows innocent passage by foreign vessels through others' territorial waters, but there is no specific term stating that military vessels have such a right." China then pointed out that several other countries agree with China on this interpretation of UNCLOS.

The Chinese government is correct that some countries have continued to argue that the rights of innocent passage guaranteed by Article 19 of UNCLOS does not apply to warships. The plain language of Article 19 ("ships of all States") suggests otherwise since the Convention specifies "warships" in other contexts when naval vessels have special treatment. But the disagreement has persisted over the years.

China's shift from complaining about U.S. violations of its sovereignty to dueling interpretations of UNCLOS reflects a possible shift in its rhetorical and diplomatic strategy. While complaining about U.S. threats to sovereignty would only highlight the aggressiveness of China's territorial claims, complaining about expansive U.S. naval operations is an issue with which other nations can find common ground with China. Indeed, China's diplomatic corps has been working overtime to line up sympathetic nations to its non-acceptance of the pending UNCLOS arbitral tribunal case brought by the Philippines. Shifting focus toward arcane interpretations of international law is better and more solid ground for China.

The United States has the better and more persuasive interpretation of UNCLOS. But if China is able to drag the United States into the technical arguments over UNCLOS, some of the political force of the U.S. FONOPs will inevitably erode. While it should not abandon FONOPs, the United States needs to come up with different ways to challenge China's land reclamations and expansionism. FONOPs are not going to be enough.

M. Taylor Fravel, Associate Professor of Political Science, MIT:
I agree with Julian about the limits of FONOPs for deterring China in the South China Sea, but for a different reason.

Put simply, FONOPs were never intended to be used as a tool in territorial or maritime jurisdictional disputes involving third parties.

The purpose of the program is limited to asserting navigational freedoms that "excessive claims" to maritime jurisdiction by other states would restrict or constrict in ways that are inconsistent with "high seas freedoms" in UNCLOS. They are operational assertions using military vessels to reinforce U.S. declaratory policy on freedom of navigation, not actions to deter how states pursue their claims in maritime disputes. By definition, FONOPs are usually a reaction to claims already made by third parties, to demonstrate that the United States does not recognize them.

> **From Beijing's perspective, FONOPs are viewed (incorrectly) as direct challenges to China's sovereignty claims and as indirect challenges to China more generally.**

In the South China Sea, FONOPs can be used to challenge excessive claims from the various land features under dispute. Recently, as Julian notes, FONOPs have been used only to challenge restrictions on the transit of military vessels through a 12 nautical mile territorial sea, such as prior permission or prior notification. Looking forward, they could be used to challenge claims to maritime jurisdiction from some artificial islands that China has created, at least four of which would not be entitled to even a territorial sea because they are artificial structures built upon a low-tide elevation.

The recent FONOPs in the South China Sea have been publicized extensively. Paradoxically, such publicity may limit further the effect of FONOPs in a third party's maritime disputes. Because they are considered to be a military operation, the Department of Defense almost never reveals the details or occurrence of particular FONOPS. Instead, they usually occur out of the public eye. The target of the operation is demarched to explain the excessive claim being challenged and a military vessel then challenges with a predetermined operation. At the end of the year, the U.S. Department of Defense publishes a report listing the countries and excessive claims that are being challenged but does not release information about individual operations.

The uncommon and unusual publicity attached to the last three FONOPs in the South China Sea represents a departure from past U.S. practice. Moreover, regarding the dynamics of the disputes in the South China Sea, such publicity may backfire, for two reasons.

First, the publicity given to these operations, widely seen as designed to challenge China, invites China to respond. From Beijing's perspective, FONOPs are viewed (incorrectly) as direct challenges to China's sovereignty claims and as indirect challenges to China more generally.

If China's leaders do not respond, they risk being viewed domestically as weak or yielding to the United States. Although China's responses have been measured and largely symbolic, the rhetoric contributes to the hardening of positions and escalation of disputes. Traditional FONOPs conducted out of the public eye would remove these incentives without weakening the content of the operational assertion.

Second, the publicity given to these recent FONOPs create strong incentives for China to emphasize its interpretations of the convention that Julian has described. Traditional FONOPs conducted out of the public eye would also remove these incentives without weakening the content of the operational assertion.

The United States should continue to perform FONOPs in the South China Sea — regularly but privately.

Malcolm Cook, Senior Fellow, Institute of Southeast Asian Studies-Yusof Ishak Institute:

Julian Ku is certainly right that U.S. freedom of navigation operations conducted under the rules of "innocent passage" will not be enough to challenge China's increasingly assertive actions on and around the disputed land features in the South China Sea. And tensions could escalate soon. If reports are correct, China's artificial island building could soon extend to Scarborough Shoal located 123 nautical miles from the main island of the Philippines, 250 nautical miles from the disputed Spratly and Paracel land features, and 530 nautical miles from China's Hainan Island. This would be a serious escalation on China's part that would likely sink the incoming Philippine administration's desire to reduce bilateral tensions over this issue, and lead to more pressure on the United States from concerned states in the region to push back against China.

Yet, the biggest shortcoming of U.S. FONOPs as a Chinese behavior-changing effort has nothing to do with the United States. The biggest problem is that the United States alone is willing to conduct these operations and suffer China's predicted and predictable backlashes.

The maritime Southeast Asian states Japan and Australia arguably have more at stake in the South China Sea but are unwilling to conduct their own operations. Maritime Southeast Asian backing for the recent U.S. operations has been ambivalent at best, and offered more in private than in public or in diplomatic forums with China present.

This, more than the widely criticized decision by the Obama administration to limit their operations to innocent passage ones, undermines the strength of the FONOPs message sent to China. The lack of active or rhetorical support from other nations undermines these operations' effectiveness in reflecting that the maritime Southeast Asian states and Japan share with the United States the conviction that China's claims to maritime rights in the South China Sea are excessive and its artificial island building activities are destabilizing. By leaving the United States alone operationally and often publicly lacking support, it allows China to dismiss these operations as simply part of U.S. efforts to contain China.

Future U.S. FONOPs in the disputed waters of the South China Sea may benefit from relaxing the innocent passage restriction, particularly in relation to China's recently constructed artificial islands. The pending ruling by the Arbitration Tribunal on the 2013 case filed by the Philippines under UNCLOS could rule that some or all of these artificial islands are constructed on low water features with no attendant territorial sea rights. However, the U.S. position in relation to the South China Sea disputes, and those of the maritime Southeast Asian states, Japan and Australia, would benefit more if the United States was not alone in conducting FONOPs. Or, at least, if support for U.S. FONOPs by these like-concerned states was more frequent, more public, and more convincing.

Print Citations

CMS: Ku, Julian G., M. Taylor Fravel, and Malcolm Cook. "Freedom of Navigation Operations in the South China Sea Aren't Enough." In *The Reference Shelf: The South China Sea Conflict*, edited by Betsy Maury, 128-131. Ipswich, MA: H.W. Wilson, 2018.

MLA: Ku, Julian G., M. Taylor Fravel, and Malcolm Cook. "Freedom of Navigation Operations in the South China Sea Aren't Enough." *The Reference Shelf: The South China Sea Conflict*. Ed. Betsy Maury. Ipswich: H.W. Wilson, 2018. 128-131. Print.

APA: Ku, J.G., M.T. Fravel, & M. Cook. (2018). Freedom of navigation operations in the South China Sea aren't enough. In Betsy Maury (Ed.), *The reference shelf: The South China Sea conflict* (pp. 128-131). Ipswich, MA: H.W. Wilson. (Original work published 2016)

Chinese Warship Seizes US Underwater Drone in International Waters

By Julian Borger
The Guardian, December 16, 2016

The Chinese navy has seized an underwater drone in plain sight of the American sailors who had deployed it in international waters, in a seemingly brazen message to the incoming Trump administration.

According to a US defence official, the unmanned glider had come to the surface of the water in the South China Sea and was about to be retrieved by the USNS *Bowditch*, an oceanographic and surveillance ship, when a Chinese naval vessel that had been shadowing the *Bowditch* put a small boat in the water.

Chinese sailors in the small boat came alongside the drone and grabbed it despite the radioed protests from the *Bowditch* that it was US property in international waters. The incident happened about 100 miles north-west of the Philippines' port of Subic Bay.

The US has issued a formal protest and demanded the return of the glider.

Peter Cook, the Pentagon press secretary, said the *Bowditch* made radio contact with the Chinese ship and asked for the glider to be returned. "The radio contact was acknowledged by the [Chinese] navy ship, but the request was ignored," Cook said.

"The UUV [unmanned underwater vehicle] is a sovereign immune vessel of the United States. We call upon China to return our UUV immediately, and to comply with all of its obligations under international law."

The aggressive Chinese gesture comes at a time of rising tensions between China and the US in the South China Sea, where Beijing has claimed ownership of a number of reefs and small islands—which it is in the process of militarising—while the US navy has been conducting patrols nearby to assert freedom of navigation in the sea lanes.

The tension has spiked since Donald Trump was elected in November. The US president-elect quickly broke a 37-year protocol by taking a call from the president of Taiwan, and openly questioned Washington's longstanding "one China" policy that does not recognise Taiwan as a separate state. Beijing has signalled it would respond dramatically if Trump implements a break in policy once he takes office on 20 January. In recent days, China has conducted bomber patrols close to Taiwan in a flexing of its military muscle.

The seizure of the drone is also a reflection of the struggle occurring under the surface of the South China Sea. As China develops a strategic submarine fleet, with the potential to carry nuclear missiles out into the Pacific Ocean, the US has built up a monitoring network designed to spot Chinese submarines as they leave their bases. Drones are key to the network, and there is a race under way between major naval powers to develop drones that can work together in swarms and "see" long distances through the water. Underwater gliders are drones that can stay underwater on the lookout for submarines for long periods of time.

"This looks like signalling from the Chinese in response to Trump's Taiwan call," said Bonnie Glaser, the director of the China Power Project at the Centre for Strategic and International Studies. "It is hard to believe this is the action of an independent commander. The Chinese now have much better control over the military, particularly the navy. It is in China's interest to send signals before Trump is inaugurated, so that he gets the message and be more restrained once he is office."

Sebastian Brixey-Williams of the British American Security Information Council said: "Nuclear states are increasing anxious about unmanned underwater vehicles (UUVs, or underwater drones) autonomously tracking their nuclear ballistic missile submarines (SSBNs), making them vulnerable to antisubmarine warfare. This is an issue for China in particular, whose SSBN fleet is small and noisy. Though the USNS

> **There is a race under way between major naval powers to develop drones that can work together in swarms and "see" long distances through the water.**

Bowditch is an oceanographic ship and may sound harmless, the kinds of data it is collecting will make Chinese submarines easier to find over time.

"China therefore accomplishes a number of things by seizing a US underwater drone," Brixey-Williams said. "It allows Chinese scientists to better understand the US's offensive technical capabilities in this area, and potentially allows them to reverse-engineer them, bringing gains in both the commercial and military spheres."

Glaser pointed out that the Chinese have frequently tested the US when there is a new administration. In the early months of the George W. Bush administration, in 2001, the Bowditch was involved in a close encounter with a Chinese frigate which turned on its gun control radar and forced it to retreat. A week later there was a collision between a US spy plane and Chinese warplane off China's Hainan island.

At about the same point in the early Obama administration, in March 2009, a number of Chinese navy ships harassed another US oceanographic vessel, the USNS *Impeccable*, coming as close as 50 ft away, trying to snag its acoustic equipment with hooks, waving flags and demanding the *Impeccable* leave the area.

Print Citations

CMS: Borger, Julian. "Chinese Warship Seizes US Underwater Drone in International Waters." In *The Reference Shelf: The South China Sea Conflict*, edited by Betsy Maury, 132-134. Ipswich, MA: H.W. Wilson, 2018.

MLA: Borger, Julian. "Chinese Warship Seizes US Underwater Drone in International Waters." *The Reference Shelf: The South China Sea Conflict*. Ed. Betsy Maury. Ipswich: H.W. Wilson, 2018. 132-134. Print.

APA: Borger, J. (2018). Chinese warship seizes US underwater drone in international waters. In Betsy Maury (Ed.), *The reference shelf: The South China Sea conflict* (pp. 132-134). Ipswich, MA: H.W. Wilson. (Original work published 2016)

Why Beijing Is Speeding Up Underwater Drone Tests in the South China Sea

By Stephen Chen
South China Morning Post, July 26, 2017

A government research vessel dropped a dozen underwater gliders at an unspecified location in the South China Sea earlier this month, Xinhua reported on Saturday. It was the biggest joint operation conducted by Chinese unmanned gliders, according to the state news agency, and comes as the US vows to step up patrols in the disputed waters.

This latest effort by China to speed up and improve collection of deep-sea data in the South China Sea for its submarine fleet operation, coincides with US President Donald Trump's reported approval of a plan to give the United States Navy more freedom to carry out patrols in the South China Sea—a move analysts say will add to uncertainties over Sino-US relations and regional security issues.

The plan, submitted to the White House in April by US defence secretary Jim Mattis, outlines a full-year schedule of when US navy ships will sail through contested waters in the South China Sea, the far-right *Breitbart News* website cited a US official as saying on Friday.

Such a move could be seen as a challenge to China's maritime claims in the disputed waters.

Yu Jiancheng, chief scientist of the expedition commissioned by the Chinese Academy of Sciences, said the 12 Haiyi (or "Sea Wing") autonomous underwater vehicles would roam for one month and collect detailed information in the ocean on a host of topics including temperature, salinity, the cleanness of water, oxygen level and the speed and direction of sea currents.

"The data is being transmitted back to a land-based laboratory in real time," meaning the information is sent out the moment it is collected under the water, Yu was quoted by Xinhua.

Yin Jingwei, dean of the college of underwater acoustic engineering at Harbin Engineering University, said that if the endeavour works as promised, "it is definitely a breakthrough".

The university, formerly known as the PLA Military Engineering Institute, developed China's first submarine. Yin was lead scientist in several military research projects on underwater communications.

"Real-time data transmission is extremely difficult for underwater gliders," he said.

Drones of this type have been used in the past year on US Navy destroyers to locate submarines, according to Western media reports. They are called gliders because they use small wings and a buoyancy control mechanism to glide down and up in the water, and wave energy to propel themselves forward.

These machines can travel long distances without needing to recharge their batteries for weeks or even months. Equipped with multiple sensors, they not only can monitor the natural environment but also can pick up data of interest to military forces, such as the propeller noise or magnetic anomaly—meaning the disturbance in the magnetic field—caused by a nuclear submarine. And because the glider produces virtually no sound, its existence can be unknown to the sub.

But American gliding drones have one weakness, according to Yin.

"They can transmit data to a mother vessel or satellite, but only when they come up to the surface," he said. This limitation can cause a time lag and discontinuity in the data stream, which can affect a military operation such as submarine tracking.

> Equipped with multiple sensors, they not only can monitor the natural environment but also can pick up data of interest to military forces, such as the propeller noise or magnetic anomaly—meaning the disturbance in the magnetic field—caused by a nuclear submarine.

Although it would be surprising if China solved the problem ahead of the US, "I cannot rule out the possibility," Yin said.

In January, China said it had built a deep-sea communications network in the western Pacific Ocean. The system allows sensors operating more than 400 metres below the surface to continuously transmit data to satellites through a grid of solar-powered buoys. Underwater data transmission can be carried out via cable or wirelessly by sound.

The Xinhua report did not say how communications among the gliders was achieved, or how far apart the drones were from one another.

Having effective communication among the gliders is important as it allows them to exchange location information that is vital for planning their movements in a region and avoiding collisions and other accidents.

"I think it could be very hard for them to spread out over a long distance," Yin said. "If they do, each must carry a powerful data transmission device. It will take the underwater communication technology to its limit."

Radio waves cannot travel in water. Long-distance underwater communication, therefore, relies almost exclusively on sound waves. But sound travels slowly, and can carry only a small amount of information.

Professor Zhu Min, a researcher with the Institute of Acoustics at the Chinese Academy of Sciences, who developed a long distance communication system for the Jiaolong, China's most powerful operating submersible capable than can take three people down to a depth of 7,000 metres, said that in water, sound travels hundreds of times slower than electromagnetic waves can in the air.

And radio waves can be sent out over high-frequency bandwidths to transmit an enormous amount of data, often in megabits or gigabits per second.

That large volume of data can be reduced to a few kilobits once in water. "The fastest sound communication in water is slower than the dial-up modem in the earliest days of the Internet," he said.

The small battery that gliders usually carry has limited power for long-distance data transmission, Zhu said. Because there is no satellite navigation system such as the Global Positioning System (GPS) or Beidou under the ocean, gliders need different technology to determine and inform one another of their whereabouts.

These technological challenges make massive deployment and coordination of underwater gliders very difficult, he said.

Thus, the Chinese underwater glider group must operate with tactics and strategy "quite different" from those of the large scale drone operation in the sky, according to the researchers.

"The underwater operation may give each glider more freedom to determine its own action due to the limited communication within the group," Zhu said. "This means the individual unit needs to be equipped with a smarter brain to deal with various situations."

Yin said that in the air, a large number of drones could be deployed to search for and zero in on one specific target. But in the water, the gliders more likely would be sent out to survey and monitor random targets within a region.

"These are different kind of approaches requiring different kind of strategic thinking," he said.

Print Citations

CMS: Chen, Stephen. "Why Beijing Is Speeding Up Underwater Drone Tests in the South China Sea." In *The Reference Shelf: The South China Sea Conflict*, edited by Betsy Maury, 135-137. Ipswich, MA: H.W. Wilson, 2018.

MLA: Chen, Stephen. "Why Beijing Is Speeding Up Underwater Drone Tests in the South China Sea." *The Reference Shelf: The South China Sea Conflict*. Ed. Betsy Maury. Ipswich: H.W. Wilson, 2018. 135-137. Print.

APA: Chen, S. (2018). Why Beijing is speeding up underwater drone tests in the South China Sea. In Betsy Maury (Ed.), *The reference shelf: The South China Sea conflict* (pp. 135-137). Ipswich, MA: H.W. Wilson. (Original work published 2017)

Thinking about Long-Term Strategy in the South China Sea

By Satoru Mori

Center for Strategic & International Studies, January 13, 2017

Most observers will agree that China has been militarizing the South China Sea, and since no country appears ready to reverse this trend by force, the shadow of China's military and paramilitary presence will grow in the years to come. Those concerned with East Asian security need to think about what the South China Sea will look like five years down the road, and consider the politico-military-economic consequences of Chinese domination of the South China Sea. Coming up with effective responses that balance strategic imperatives with political considerations is key to dealing with China in the South China Sea.

Consequences of Chinese Dominance and Unilateralism in the South China Sea

What are the consequences of Chinese bases in the South China Sea? What is the South China Sea going to look like in the years to come? As recent Features from AMTI show, China has turned its artificial islands into fortified outposts that could readily serve paramilitary and military purposes. China could assign multiple functions to these bases to cause the following consequences:

First, these bases could replenish maritime law enforcement and maritime militia vessels, allowing China to impose what it deems "domestic jurisdiction and regulation" more rigorously. China could declare "economic zones" where it does not hold legitimate maritime claims, and block foreign fishing vessels from operating in those areas. Chinese maritime law enforcement authorities and/or maritime militia could easily scare off foreign fishermen by arresting or otherwise punishing them. If foreign governments respond with nothing more than diplomatic protests, Chinese fishing vessels would have a virtually free hand to monopolize fishery resources in the South China Sea. China could also harass foreign marine transportation vessels on the grounds of violating some Chinese "domestic regulation" in its self-claimed maritime areas. While the motivation would be political, China could use technical-legal reasons to apply economic pressure on foreign governments whose states rely on freedom of navigation in the South China Sea.

Second, China would be able to expand its surveillance and reconnaissance activities during peacetime by using these bases as supply and refueling points for naval and air patrol assets, providing the People's Liberation

> **Those concerned with East Asian security need to think about what the South China Sea will look like five years down the road, and consider the politico-military-economic consequences of Chinese domination of the South China Sea.**

Army (PLA) enhanced capability to monitor and detect U.S. and foreign military activities in the region. A PLA that could more effectively harass normal activities of foreign military units (see the recent seizure of a U.S. unmanned undersea vehicle) would make it increasingly difficult for the U.S. and other militaries to monitor Chinese activities, especially in the undersea domain. Peacetime competition to establish and enhance air and maritime domain awareness would shift in China's favor. China would be better able to declare and regulate a South China Sea air defense identification zone.

Third, China could use these bases to sustain low-intensity military operations. Experts have pointed out in the past that these islands could easily be demolished if a war were to break out between China and the United States, and that would be correct in the event of a full-fledged war that involved kinetic operations against military bases. However, skirmishes and conflicts on the seas and over isolated land features could remain at the lower range of the conventional conflict spectrum. Protracted standoff situations would be more of a competition of continuous reinforcement and replenishment on the seas. With these resupply bases so close to potential conflict areas, China would have a distinct advantage in sustaining military pressure for the duration of any protracted maritime confrontations. In short, its island bases provide China with escalation dominance in individual standoff incidents at sea.

The above effects, taken together, would create Chinese regional hegemony. Some observers believe that China is isolating itself, but China appears to disagree. From a Chinese perspective, the countries that it pushed away during the course of expansion will return to its orbit once its dominance is realized, and it may in fact feel that this is already happening. At some point in the future, China is likely to choose a moment to demonstrate its might, and thereby generate the perception that it dominates the South China Sea.

A Framework for a Long-Term Strategy for the South China Sea

What would be the ends, ways, and means constituting a long-term strategy for the South China Sea?

The goal of such a strategy would be to deter armed conflict and maintain an environment where states are able to fully exercise and enjoy their rights guaranteed under the United Nations Convention on the Law of the Sea (UNCLOS). The ways of realizing this goal would involve enhancing conventional deterrence whereby major states like the United States, Japan, Australia, India, and even seafaring

European nations would systematically provide military and paramilitary capacity-building programs to Southeast Asian nations through a maritime security policy coordination mechanism, and calibrate relations with China whenever it violates fundamental norms like peaceful resolution of disputes in the South China Sea. Some methods of achieving the above might include:

1. *Further enhancing U.S. military presence through joint training and exercises, freedom of navigation operations, regular patrols, and forward deployment.*

2. *Expanding arms exports to Southeast Asian nations.* Although foreign military sales are competitive in nature, the overall approach of arms-exporting states should be coordinated as much as possible and also incorporate a competitive strategy perspective geared toward providing various military capabilities to coastal states of the South China Sea. Provision of buyer's credit to Southeast Asian nations could facilitate and accelerate capability enhancement of regional states.

3. *Engaging primate companies to expand and enhance capacity-building programs for Southeast Asian states' maritime law enforcement authorities.* U.S. or multinational private maritime security companies—hired by local governments that are financially assisted by countries like the United States and Japan—could provide both training to local maritime law enforcement units and escorts for local fishing vessels that operate in China's self-claimed maritime zones. U.S. and local military surveillance units could watch over escorted fishing activities, and warn and record the actions of Chinese maritime militia or law enforcement units whenever they harass foreign fishing vessels that are engaged in legitimate and lawful fishing activities. Escort activities by U.S. or multinational private maritime security companies would allow the United States and other countries to inject their presence at the paramilitary level in the South China Sea. Manned by former maritime law enforcement professionals, equipped with large vessels, and rapidly and selectively deployable, private maritime security units could potentially alleviate the paramilitary imbalance between China and other coastal states.

4. *Concluding a multilateral maritime security cooperation agreement between Southeast Asian states in need of maritime security assistance and the United States, Japan, Australia, and other states willing to preserve the freedom of the seas.* The agreement should not include a mutual defense clause. Rather, it should establish a policy dialogue mechanism devoted to maritime security that would address issues concerning coordinated arms exports and capacity-building as mentioned above. In contrast to the current indirect, piecemeal approach, this coordination mechanism would enable systematic and coordinated capacity-building programs to advance with a clearer blueprint in the process of building conventional and law enforcement capabilities of regional states. The agreement could cover a number of important facets including maritime information-sharing among member states, and emergency financial/economic assistance to those that face economic reprisal or pressure from a

non-party state. The mechanism could serve also as a diplomatic platform—whenever a member state encountered the use of paramilitary or military force that violated rights guaranteed under UNCLOS in the South China Sea, the member states would denounce such acts with one voice, and consider the possibility of coordinated response whenever possible.

Print Citations

CMS: Mori, Satoru. "Thinking about Long-Term Strategy in the South China Sea." In *The Reference Shelf: The South China Sea Conflict*, edited by Betsy Maury, 138-141. Ipswich, MA: H.W. Wilson, 2018.

MLA: Mori, Satoru. "Thinking about Long-Term Strategy in the South China Sea." *The Reference Shelf: The South China Sea Conflict*. Ed. Betsy Maury. Ipswich: H.W. Wilson, 2018. 138-141. Print.

APA: Mori, S. (2018). Thinking about long-term strategy in the South China Sea. In Betsy Maury (Ed.), *The reference shelf: The South China Sea conflict* (pp. 138-141). Ipswich, MA: H.W. Wilson. (Original work published 2017)

6
Sovereignty and Codes of Conduct

Photo by Aaron Favila/AFP/Getty Images

Chinese Foreign Minister Wang Yi (5th L) links arms with ASEAN Foreign Ministers during the 50th Association of Southeast Asian Nations (ASEAN) regional security forum in suburban Manila on August 6, 2017. The annual forum, hosted by ASEAN, brings together the top diplomats from 26 countries and the European Union for talks on political and security issues in Asia-Pacific.

Ownership of the Sea: Sovereignty and Territorial Conduct

In political philosophy, the term "sovereignty" refers to the right of a government, or leader, or a nation as a unit, to exercise control over the peoples and territories lying within their boundaries. Determining sovereignty is at the heart of the South China Sea conflict for the coastal nations involved and the determination of sovereignty has broader international implications. Military control of the islands in the sea does not currently follow the rules of United National Convention on the Law of the Sea (UNCLOS), with China, Vietnam, and the Philippines claiming islands that would, under UNCLOS, be within the territorial seas or exclusive economic zones (EEZs) of other nations. International law can guide the sovereignty debate, but has not proven an effective tool for solving the conflict. A more promising effort, still underway, involves bilateral negotiation between the nations bordering the sea and the potential for the Association of South East Asian Nations (ASEAN) to develop an effective regional agreement that might settle or postpone determinations of sovereignty in favor of deeper cooperative agreements.

Sovereignty in International Law

Sovereignty is a complex and controversial subject in political philosophy and law. Modern concepts of sovereignty can be traced to the development of a European "sovereign state" system, resulting in the Peace of Westphalia in 1698, a series of treaties between the cities of Osnabrück and Münster that ended the Thirty Years' War (1618 to 1648). The concept of sovereignty that was developed in the peace agreement became integrated into Western European expansionism and thus into the laws of the societies that emerged from Europe's colonial period. Sovereignty thus became, for centuries, a foundation of international law and the formation of treaties and agreements.[1]

There is no single definition accepted around the world of what constitutes a sovereign state. There is a constitutive theory of statehood, which says, for a state to be sovereign, it must be recognized as sovereign by at least one other recognized state. By contrast, the declarative theory holds that all a state needs to be sovereign is to control a physical territory, to demonstrate a permanent population, to have a government of some form, and to have the ability to enter into relations with other entities. However, some formulations of international law only recognize a declarative state as sovereign if the state did not form through military conquest.[2]

The world is composed of both recognized states and "unrecognized states," which are entities that have developed an internal concept of statehood, but that are not recognized by external powers. Taiwan is a classic example, as the self-governing island typically considers itself a separate nation, but is considered a wholly owned territory by the Republic of China. The long-standing sovereignty dispute between the two societies has continued into the 2010s, with some Taiwanese leaders, and other countries, recognizing Taiwan as a separate state while others, fearful of angering China, have deferred to mainland China's claims of ownership.[3]

The gradual advance of globalism eroded the concept of sovereignty with regard to the rights of the state in regard to the treatment of citizens. The horrors of the genocidal Nazi campaign during World War II were sufficient to motivate state leaders to develop international principles with regard to human rights. The United Nations itself is, in fact and in many ways, an anti-sovereign entity though the international law developed through the UN and regional partnerships also bolsters and creates legal guidelines for the establishment and maintenance of sovereign rights. Membership in the United Nations requires states to relinquish (at least in principal) some degree of freedom with regard to their sovereign powers and properties. In 1948, the vast majority of UN nations signed the Universal Declaration of Human Rights, committing to recognize 30 separate individual rights and not to circumscribe or violate those rights during the administration of their governments. The declaration was not legally binding and provided no penalties for nations that failed to adhere, but it is notable as a first, early effort to bind UN countries to a shared set of principles regarding beneficent governance.[4]

Over time, the United Nations matured, and member nations participated in developing stronger agreements, tied to economic incentives and potential penalties, designed to encourage and, in some cases, force, states to adhere to UN conventions. Economic sanctions, expulsion from treaties and multinational groups, and even joint military intervention have been used to penalize states for violating UN laws. As membership in the United Nations and other international governing groups came to include more substantial benefits in the form of trade and mutual assistance agreements, expulsion from the United Nations also became a more significant threat. Finally, the United Nations has intervened in human rights conflicts around the world, drawing from member countries to provide military and humanitarian aid to communities in crisis.

Critics of the UN and other international organizations sometimes argue that such endeavors are typically highly flawed and ineffective. For one thing, international organizations can tie nations together in such a way that one nation may suffer from the mismanagement of another. Participation in international law also typically involves extensive debate over extended periods before action is taken on an issue, while a single state, or a state engaged in a far-simpler bilateral agreement, may address issues more effectively over the short term. The 2010s has seen something of a backlash against the gradual globalization of law, as seen in China's refusal to adhere to UNCLOS in the South China Sea, but also in the Trump administration's abandonment of UN climate change agreements, and the Brexit vote that will see the UK exit the European Union. While smaller nations are often more closely tethered by the need for international agreements to enhance defense and build economic stability, such nations tend to be more invested in international law.

By contrast, the largest and most powerful nations, like Russia, the United States, India, Japan, and China, are more likely to pick and choose which aspects of international government they wish to uphold.

Sovereignty in the South China Sea

Writing in *Huffington Post*, Chinese Professor of International Studies Shen Dingli argues that international law does not prohibit the reclamation of land or islands from the sea. Shen notes that the United States has had little reaction to similar activities undertaken by Vietnam in the same sea, or by Japan on the Okinotori Islands, even though Japan used its dredging to demand a new EEZ, despite the fact that UNCLOS support this claim. Shen thus argues that US policy in the region is not consistent with a broad commitment to international law, but rather, a reflection of competition with China.[5]

In 2016, the UN ruled that China did not have any legitimate, existing claims to sovereignty to most of the territories claimed by China in the South China Sea, and, in fact, the UN validated historical claims made by Vietnam on the basis that the Vietnamese inherited sovereignty from France after France had established sovereign control over many of the contested islands during the French occupation of Vietnam. China does not dispute this, and accepts that China recognized French sovereignty during the colonial era, but argues that Vietnam subsequently recognized China's sovereignty over the islands in return for Chinese assistance during the Vietnam conflict. Thus, China argues that their claim is consistent with international law regarding sovereignty, in that the nation's control of the islands was recognized by other sovereign nations most recently. The UN found this claim unconvincing in that China had mismanaged the island territories, to the detriment of all nations, had unlawfully restricted access to open waters, and had occupied islands within the EEZs of other nations.

The United States cannot take a direct stance on sovereignty. This is, in part, because the United States has military and commercial interests in territories contested by multiple parties. For instance, Thitu Island, controlled by the Philippines, has been suggested as a potential site for a US military base, but the island is also claimed by Vietnam, Taiwan, and China. Therefore, by taking sides in the issue, the United States not only sides against China's aggressive policy, but also against the claims made by other states, states with whom the United States has mutual pacts and agreements. Further, by occupying an island or rock with contested sovereignty, the United States would venture into uncertain legal ground, with all of the contesting claimants within their rights, until sovereignty is internationally established, to take military action. While this is perhaps unlikely, it is not a strategy likely to result in easing tensions in the region.[6]

Regional Organizations and Codes of Conduct

For many years, the Philippines was the strongest opponent of China's activities in the South China Sea. However, the 2016 election of Rodrigo Duterte signaled the end of this movement within the nation. Duterte continued to give vocal support for Philippine claims in the sea, but also stated after his election that he would table the issue, despite the UN ruling in favor of the Philippines over China, in favor of bilateral negotiations with Chinese leaders.

One possibility for easing tensions in the region is through negotiation within the Association of South East Asian Nations (ASEAN). ASEAN is a regional inter-governmental group that includes all of the direct claimants in the South China Sea Controversy as well as a number of other Southeast Asian Nations without coastal claims but that are equally invested in preserving peace in the region. The 2002 summit of ASEAN nations resulted in a Conduct of Parties in the South China Sea document (DOC), which was never fully implemented after it was drafted be-cause of disagreements between member nations over whether or not the docu-ment should be legally binding. As a result, the nations accepted the document as a temporary measure, and agreed to revisit the legality of the DOC at a later date. As tensions increased, after China's territorial expansion became more aggressive, a legally binding agreement failed to cohere.

At the 2017 31st ASEAN Summit in Manila, Chinese leaders announced that the committee would be attempting to formulate a Code of Conduct (COC) for the South China Sea, though China did not commit to a legally binding agreement. Philippine Foreign Secretary Alan Peter Ceyetano also stated that the Philippines would prefer a nonlegal document. Whether this means that a new COC will also lack any penalties for nations that violate the code is unclear. Since the controversy intensified in 2015, China has made direct overtures to the Philippines, Vietnam, and Malaysia, offering bilateral agreements in return for acceptance, temporarily, of China's territorial expansion. For instance, when visiting Vietnam in 2017, Chinese President Xi Jinping offered Vietnam 12 separate cooperation pacts and $1.94 bil-lion worth of economic deals and assistance, in return for Vietnam's agreement to work towards a bilateral agreement on the two nations' territorial disagreements.[7]

Whether or not bilateral or regional negotiation will result in major changes in the South China Sea remains unclear. China is the economic leader of ASEAN and is capable, economically and militarily, of bending other nations to its will. If prog-ress towards settling the South China Sea dispute occurs solely through ASEAN or direct bilateral efforts between Asian nations, broader global interests are less likely to be served and China's territorial expansion is thus more likely to proceed in its current form. There remains, however, room for the United States and other peripheral nations, like Australia and Japan, to influence the ASEAN process and to engage in the same type of deal making that China has used to promote its own interests. The involvement of the US in such efforts, however, depends on what Donald Trump's "America first" policy means for US policy in Asia. The Trump administration has been wary of international agreements, has claimed that US in-volvement in global government has been detrimental to the United States, despite objections from economists and historians on this point. If this strategy means that the US is unwilling to engage in the same kind of deal-brokering as China, this might mean that the role for the US in the South China Sea conflict will be limited in the coming years.

Micah L. Issitt

Works Used

Caspersen, Nina. *Unrecognized States: The Struggle for Sovereignty in the Modern International System*. Malden, MA: Polity Press, 2012.

Crawford, James R. *The Creation of States in International Law (2nd ed)*. New York: Oxford University Press, 2007.

Croxton, Derek. "The Peace of Westphalia of 1648 and the Origins of Sovereignty." *The International History Review*. Vol. 21, No. 3 (Sep. 1999), 569.

Ku, Julian. "Why the U.S. Can't Take Sides in South China Sea Sovereignty Disputes, Even against China." *Lawfare*. Lawfare Institute. Jun 19 2017. Web. 18 Dec 2017.

Lee, YingHui. "A South China Sea Code of Conduct: Is Real Progress Possible?" *The Diplomat*. Nov 18 2017. Web. 18 Dec 2017.

Shen, Dingli. "Why China Has the Right to 'Build Sovereignty' in the South China Sea." *Huffington Post*. The World Post. 2017. Web. 18 Dec 2017.

"Sovereignty." *Plato.stanford*. Stanford Encyclopedia of Philosophy. Mar 25 2016. Web. 18 Dec 2017.

Notes

1. Croxton, "The Peace of Westphalia of 1648 and the Origins of Sovereignty."
2. Crawford, *The Creation of States in International Law (2nd ed)*.
3. Caspersen, *Unrecognized States: The Struggle for Sovereignty in the Modern International System*.
4. "Sovereignty," *Plato.stanford*.
5. Shen, "Why China Has the Right to 'Build Sovereignty' in the South China Sea."
6. Ku, "Why the U.S. Can't Take Sides in the South China Sea Sovereignty Disputes, Even against China."
7. Lee, "A South China Sea Code of Conduct: Is Real Progress Possible?"

China and the United States: A Conversation with David M. Lampton

The Asia Foundation, July 26, 2015

Prof. Lampton spoke with us recently in Beijing about current U.S.-China relations, in anticipation of the first state visit by China's President Xi Jinping to the United States, later this fall. Here is an edited version of that conversation.

With rising tensions over issues like the South China Sea and cybersecurity, and increasingly negative rhetoric between the United States and China, how can the two sides find common ground and get their strategic relationship back on track? We have to start from the premise that two big countries at different economic levels and with very different histories will never have perfectly smooth relations. Our aspiration has to be to manage this relationship well. We've effectively managed this relationship for 40 years, and I believe it can be managed for another 40 years if we have wise leaders in both countries.

There are a number of ways to manage this relationship. We're China's biggest export market; China's our most rapidly growing large export market. We're economically interdependent. We have to build our relationship on interdependence. One of the ways to do that is to invest more heavily in each other's country. Under current circumstances, 200,000 to 400,000 Americans will be working in Chinese-owned manufacturing and other enterprises in the United States by 2020. When you employ people, they then have a personal stake in the relationship. I think the outward policy of China in investing in the United States is very good and should be encouraged. Many people have the impression that the United States is one of the biggest investors in China. That's actually not true, so there's a lot more room for investment in both directions.

Secondly, our leaders are already engaged in dialogue. They are now in regular, direct conversation. They are getting together on a regular basis – sometimes more than twice a year in meetings like APEC. So dialogue between top leaders is essential.

Many people will speak to the good news of increasing military exchanges. That's true. But overall, the character of the military-to-military relationship is deteriorating. We need to do what we can to halt that. That brings us to the South China Sea. It's a complicated issue, but the basic problem is that China's neighbors are becoming increasingly anxious about China's growing role in the region, military and otherwise. Somehow, China needs to reassure its neighbors and solve or shelve these maritime issues as earlier PRC leaders did.

While China has to be more reassuring to its neighbors, the United States has to be clear that it welcomes China having a greater voice in the world. China was poorer than Cambodia when Mao Zedong died. Now it's the second largest economy in the world. And yet China's voting share in the International Monetary Fund is only 3.8 percent. So the U.S. has to be more willing to make room for China in international organizations as appropriate to its status.

For both sides, domestic politics are at a very sensitive stage. In the U.S., we have presidential elections. In China, the 19th Party Congress is coming up. Five out of the seven Standing Committee members will retire. There will undoubtedly be some jockeying over what the complexion of the new government will be. There will be politics.

When there's political competition, people talk tough when they're talking about foreigners. You have two societies that don't want to appear weak to their own people. That's a problem. So we have to manage that. If we don't manage it well, or tolerably well, then what's the consequence of that? Having the world's biggest economy fight with the second biggest economy is not a way to solve any problem. If we have rational leadership in both capitals, we'll find a way through.

China's President Xi Jinping is heading to Washington D.C. this fall for his first state visit to the United States. President Barack Obama's trip to China last year resulted in a major climate agreement. Do you anticipate any key breakthroughs during Xi's trip? In your view, what would make this a successful visit?
We make a mistake when we judge the success of a trip or any leadership interaction solely by the "deliverables," or tangible agreements. It's important to have some agreements, but they should be few in number, and important and strategic in character. More fundamentally, if you ask, "What's the core problem of U.S.-China relations?" it's basically that the two peoples don't trust each other. That's the beginning of the problem. So if that's the undergirding problem, then you want to measure the trip by how it contributes to reducing that problem. Therefore, I would define the goal to be "make friends."

This will be Xi Jinping's first visit to the U.S. as head of state. But he came as vice president in February 2012. And he visited Muscatine, Iowa, in 1985. That was tremendously popular. First of all, it brought him into contact with real people. Secondly, local media paid a lot of attention. Frankly, national media are pretty critical all the time. But local media and local political figures are much more concerned with economic development, tourism, and exports of soybeans. So he could speak to issues that were intrinsically meaningful to the people he was speaking to. Beijing ought to define its job as how to relate in a meaningful way to our citizens. Of course, they have to talk to Congress, respective foreign ministries, etc. But they ought to give equal weight to simply trying to connect with people.

On a more substantive front, the upcoming summit, there will be an agreement to move further forward on climate change. That would be important. That will be one of the major security concerns of both countries for the next 50 to 100 years. I would expect that they would move forward with discussion of a bilateral investment treaty. The main issue for the United States is how many sectors of China's economy will be declared open by definition.

They will probably agree to do more on military-to-military exchanges. That's good and important. The fact is, however, that as long as Beijing and Tokyo have tension over the Diaoyu/Senkaku Islands, that brings Washington into alignment with Japan, which worries China. And as long as China expands its presence in the South China Sea, that brings it into conflict with its neighbors and a U.S. that worries about coercion, navigation, and international law. For its part, Beijing is aggravated by significant U.S. surveillance close in to its shores. Until each side changes its behavior, you won't see a genuinely improved U.S.-China military relationship.

You have publicly warned that the U.S.-China relationship is at a critical "tipping point." From your perspective as a longtime China watcher, what do you think about the future trajectory of bilateral relations?
I said we were approaching a tipping point. I didn't say we had gone off the cliff. I don't know if we're five feet, five yards, or five miles from that point, but we're a lot closer to it than I'd like to be.

For the 40-plus years since Nixon went to China, and certainly since Deng Xiaoping came back to power in 1977, most Americans have seen China as going in the "right direction" in terms of foreign and domestic policy—with ups and downs, to be sure. 1989 raised questions. But Deng Xiaoping and George H. W. Bush got ties modestly back on track. China was opening up, investing in the world. Most Americans saw China as moving in the right direction. Conversely, most Chinese saw the U.S. as basically moving in the right direction in terms of policy towards China.

Somewhere around 2008 to 2010, each side began to wonder about the direction of the other. With the rise of South China Sea problems, Diaoyu, and anti-Japanese demonstrations, many Americans weren't so sure China was going in the right direction, particularly during the global financial crisis. Americans were worried about their economic future. China had a very big trade surplus. It seemed that China was successful

> **While China has to be more reassuring to its neighbors, the United States has to be clear that it welcomes China having a greater voice in the world.**

but at the same time was going the wrong way in terms of foreign and domestic policy. I think most Americans are approaching the point where they believe it's going the wrong way for us. The election coming up is going to give voice to that.

In China, one of the first questions they ask is, "Why is the U.S. trying to keep China down or contain China?" One of the major things pushing this is: when you have positive expectations for the future, you then have positive policies and you subordinate frictions, because the long term is going to be better. But if you think the future is going to be worse, you fall into a threatening posture; you're not willing to overlook current frictions. Mentally, where the two peoples currently are is not a healthy place.

We're moving from a relationship that was trying to find partnership to one now of deterrence. And threats are a key part of that. China has one aircraft carrier, is building another one for sure, and maybe a third one. China is putting military capability on some of these island reclamation projects in the South China Sea. China's recent military White Paper said the PRC was going to build a more seaworthy, power-projection navy. And the U.S., with the Pivot announcement in 2011, rotating troops—small forces—through Australia, and tightening up our alliance structure with Japan, all that creates anxiety in Beijing. Now we've got joint exercises with Australia, Japan, and the Philippines. These are worrisome developments for China. So what you see is that we're each reacting to the other. The relationship is becoming fundamentally more competitive. My feeling about this tipping point is that psychologically, both our people are going in the wrong direction. And the underlying security relationship is deteriorating. My remarks on the tipping point weren't so much to criticize one party or the other, but were more of a call to say, "Let's address the real problem."

As chairman of the board of The Asia Foundation, do you have any thoughts about how the Chinese government can effectively hold the nonprofit sector to account while enabling domestic and foreign NGOs to continue carrying out useful programs in China?
China should have a regulatory framework for organizations. The question is, how to regulate them? There are two mechanisms: (1) Auditing procedures. Everyone should be accountable for how they are spending their money, because, by nature, these are public service organizations, and, of course, spending should be for lawful, public purposes. The state has a legitimate function in ascertaining where NGOs are getting their money and where it's going. (2) Governance of organizations. You should have a board of directors. They should be empowered to make a certain range of decisions, and be responsible for the broad performance of organizations within the bounds of legal, public purposes and fiduciary responsibility.

However, when you have too broad a definition of security and begin to infringe on all the programs, that's going overboard. That will have the consequence of many organizations leaving China. It will harm the fabric of civil relations between our two countries—and with other foreign countries—and harm mutual understanding. The process of oversight shouldn't be so complicated, intrusive, and exacting that organizations can't function. You need a governance structure, an accountability structure, but don't micromanage these organizations. If we look at the reaction to the draft overseas NGO law, the response from around the world has been one of disquiet, and I hope the Chinese government will listen.

Print Citations

CMS: "China and the United States: A Conversation with David M. Lampton." In *The Reference Shelf: The South China Sea Conflict*, edited by Betsy Maury, 151-155. Ipswich, MA: H.W. Wilson, 2018.

MLA: "China and the United States: A Conversation with David M. Lampton." *The Reference Shelf: The South China Sea Conflict*. Ed. Betsy Maury. Ipswich: H.W. Wilson, 2018. 151-155. Print.

APA: The Asia Foundation. (2018). China and the United States: A conversation with David M. Lampton. In Betsy Maury (Ed.), *The reference shelf: The South China Sea conflict* (pp. 151-155). Ipswich, MA: H.W. Wilson. (Original work published 2015)

Good Fences or Good Neighbours in the South China Sea

By Sam Bateman

East Asia Forum, August 18, 2016

Despite the old adage that 'good fences make good neighbours', sometimes it is impossible, for a variety of reasons, to build good 'fences' in the sea. This is certainly the case in the South China Sea, where territorial claims are complicated by geography.

While the recent ruling by the Arbitral Tribunal in The Hague on the dispute between China and the Philippines in the South China Sea has theoretically 'cleared the air' on some aspects of maritime boundary-making, in practical terms it may not have helped the situation.

The surprising feature of the ruling was the judgment that there are no 'fully entitled' islands in the Spratly group. There are numerous ramifications of this judgment, including for the status of other islands in the South China Sea. Islands in both the Paracel and Pratas groups are much larger than in the Spratlys and likely to satisfy the criteria to be regarded as 'fully entitled' islands. But maritime boundaries near the Paracels cannot be defined while sovereignty over this group is disputed between China and Vietnam.

Theoretically the ruling that there are only 'rocks' in the Spratlys provides a basis for a system of exclusive economic zone (EEZ) boundaries in the South China Sea with a number of enclaved territorial seas around the 'rocks'. There may even be a resulting patch of high seas that are uncontested, although this may be closed off in part by the outer continental shelf claims by Vietnam and Malaysia.

> A cooperative management regime is the only solution to the problems of the South China Sea.

Vietnam could also help 'clear the air', as well as bolster ASEAN solidarity, by dropping its claim to features within the EEZs of Malaysia and the Philippines.

The importance the Tribunal attached to EEZ jurisdiction may reinforce the nationalistic attitude the littoral states attach to their EEZs. They will be looking for 'fences in the sea' rather than recognising that maritime boundaries are not an end in themselves but rather a means of effectively managing maritime space. This should be the basic objective of all the littoral states to the South China Sea. It is also their obligation under Part IX of the United Nations Convention on the Law of the Sea (UNCLOS) in terms of cooperating in semi-enclosed seas.

There are other issues that complicate maritime boundary agreements in the South China Sea. Negotiation and adoption of a maritime boundary is fundamentally political, and the politics of maritime boundary-making restricts effective governance of the South China Sea. A country's negotiators will be influenced by national sentiment and reluctant to concede sovereignty over maritime space that the community regards, rightly or wrongly, as part of their own country.

Unfortunately this is the situation now in the South China Sea, with the national media of claimant countries, including the Chinese media, giving wide coverage to the disputes. The recent ruling may reinforce these sentiments.

Another issue in determining maritime boundaries in the South China Sea is whether or not EEZs should coincide with continental shelf boundaries. Different approaches to this issue are evident around the world, depending as much as anything on the state of the bilateral relationship between the neighbouring countries. If the relationship is sound, overlapping jurisdiction may be feasible, but if it is not, the parties are unlikely to achieve the necessary level of agreement and cooperation.

While the general trend is to have coincident continental shelf and EEZ boundaries, this is not always possible, and states with overlapping claims may adopt separate boundaries for their EEZ and the continental shelf. This may be the case where a continental shelf boundary was agreed, largely on the basis of geological considerations, prior to wide acceptance of the EEZ regime under UNCLOS.

This issue is already a problem in the South China Sea where Indonesia and Malaysia have agreed on a continental shelf boundary east of the Natuna islands, but no EEZ boundary. Malaysia wants the EEZ and continental shelf boundaries to coincide, but this is opposed by Indonesia. Similarly, Indonesia and Vietnam have agreed on a continental shelf boundary but no EEZ boundary.

The South China Sea situation will only be settled when the bordering countries change their mindsets from one of sovereignty, sole ownership of resources and seeking 'fences in the sea' to one of functional cooperation and cooperative management.

A cooperative management regime is the only solution to the problems of the South China Sea. The most acceptable framework for a new regime would be a web of provisional arrangements covering cooperation for different functions with perhaps even different areas for each function.

These functions could include joint development of oil and gas resources, fisheries management, marine safety, marine scientific research, good order at sea, and preservation and protection of the marine environment. Regardless of whether or not maritime boundaries are agreed, urgent safety, resource and environmental problems dictate the need for increased dialogue and cooperation.

Print Citations

CMS: Bateman, Sam. "Good Fences or Good Neighbours in the South China Sea." In *The Reference Shelf: The South China Sea Conflict*, edited by Betsy Maury, 156-158. Ipswich, MA: H.W. Wilson, 2018.

MLA: Bateman, Sam. "Good Fences or Good Neighbours in the South China Sea." *The Reference Shelf: The South China Sea Conflict*. Ed. Betsy Maury. Ipswich: H.W. Wilson, 2018. 156-158. Print.

APA: Bateman, S. (2018). Good fences or good neighbours in the South China Sea. In Betsy Maury (Ed.), *The reference shelf: The South China Sea conflict* (pp. 156-158). Ipswich, MA: H.W. Wilson. (Original work published 2016)

ASEAN, China Adopt[s] [a] Framework for Crafting [a] Code on South China Sea

By Christian Shepherd and Manuel Mogato
Reuters, August 6, 2017

MANILA (Reuters)—Foreign ministers of Southeast Asia and China adopted on Sunday a negotiating framework for a code of conduct in the South China Sea, a move they hailed as progress but seen by critics as [a] tactic to buy China time to consolidate its maritime power.

The framework seeks to advance a 2002 Declaration of Conduct (DOC) of Parties in the South China Sea, which has mostly been ignored by claimant states, particularly China, which has built seven manmade islands in disputed waters, three of which are equipped with runways, surface-to-air missiles and radars.

All parties say the framework is only an outline for how the code will be established but critics say the failure to outline as an initial objective the need to make the code legally binding and enforceable, or have a dispute resolution mechanism, raises doubts about how effective the pact will be.

Chinese Foreign Minister Wang Yi said the adoption of the framework created a solid foundation for negotiations that could start this year, if "the situation in the South China Sea is generally stable and on the premise that there is no major interference from outside parties."

He told reporters there had been "really tangible progress" so there was "a need to cherish momentum on the South China Sea".

Signing China up to a legally binding and enforceable code for the strategic waterway has long been a goal for claimant members of the Association of South East Asian Nations (ASEAN), some of which have sparred for years over what they see as China's disregard for their sovereign rights and its blocking of fishermen and energy exploration efforts.

Beijing insists its activities are for defense purposes, in areas it considers its waters. Malaysia, Taiwan, Brunei, Vietnam and the Philippines, however, all claim some or all of the South China Sea and its myriad shoals, reefs and islands.

Some critics and diplomats believe China's sudden interest in the code after 15 years of delays is to drag out the negotiating process to buy time to complete its strategic objectives in the South China Sea, through which more than $3 billion of ship-borne trade passes annually.

Weaker Hand

Opponents also say it is being pushed through at a time when the United States, long seen as a crucial buffer against China's maritime assertiveness, is distracted by other issues and providing no real clarity about its security strategy in Asia, thus weakening ASEAN's bargaining position.

> The framework seeks to advance a 2002 Declaration of Conduct (DOC) of Parties in the South China Sea, which has mostly been ignored by claimant states, particularly China, which has built seven manmade islands in disputed waters, three of which as equipped with runways, surface-to-air missiles and radars.

The framework has not been made public but a leaked two-page blueprint seen by Reuters is broad and leaves wide scope for disagreement.

It urges a commitment to the "purposes and principles" of the United Nations Convention on the Law of the Sea (UNCLOS) but does not specify adherence to it, for example.

A separate ASEAN document, dated May and seen by Reuters, shows that Vietnam pushed for stronger, more specific text in the framework, wanting mention of a dispute resolution mechanism and respecting "sovereignty, sovereign rights and jurisdiction".

Sovereign rights cover entitlements to fish and extraction of natural resources.

Several ASEAN countries, including Vietnam and the Philippines, have said they still favor making the code legally binding, something experts say China is unlikely to agree to.

Wang said he would not try to anticipate what the code will comprise, but said whatever is signed must be adhered to.

Robespierre Bolivar, foreign ministry spokesman of host Philippines, said the adoption of the framework symbolised the commitment to creating a "substantive and effective" code.

Print Citations

CMS: Shepherd, Christian, and Manuel Mogato. "ASEAN, China Adopt[s] [a] Framework for Crafting [a] Code on South China Sea." In *The Reference Shelf: The South China Sea Conflict*, edited by Betsy Maury, 159-161. Ipswich, MA: H.W. Wilson, 2018.

MLA: Shepherd, Christian, and Manuel Mogato. "ASEAN, China Adopt[s] [a] Framework for Crafting [a] Code on South China Sea." *The Reference Shelf: The South China Sea Conflict*. Ed. Betsy Maury. Ipswich: H.W. Wilson, 2018. 159-161. Print.

APA: Shepherd, C., & M. Mogato. (2018). ASEAN, China adopt[s] [a] framework for crafting [a] code on South China Sea. In Betsy Maury (Ed.), *The reference shelf: The South China Sea conflict* (pp. 159-161). Ipswich, MA: H.W. Wilson. (Original work published 2017)

How China Views the South China Sea: As Sovereign Territory

By Dean Cheng

The Heritage Foundation, **November 5, 2015**

With the decision to conduct a Freedom of Navigation Operation (FONOP) in the waters around China's artificial islands in the South China Sea, U.S.-Chinese relations appear set to deteriorate in the coming year. Given the likely rise in tensions, especially if the United States conducts additional FONOPS, it is essential that U.S. leaders understand the Chinese perspective, even as they must make clear to Beijing (and others) that they are firmly committed to the principle of freedom of the seas.

Some have attempted to explain China's approach by comparing it to the Monroe Doctrine. China, they say, is intent on asserting a sphere of influence, in which its interests are accorded primacy.

We should expect China to devise its own version of the Monroe Doctrine, as imperial Japan did in the 1930s. In fact, we are already seeing inklings of that policy. For example, Chinese leaders have made it clear they do not think the United States has a right to interfere in disputes over the maritime boundaries of the South China Sea, a strategically important body of water that Beijing effectively claims as its own.

An alternative analogy often drawn likens China to either imperial, Wilhelmine or even Nazi Germany. In this portrayal, China is intent upon expanding its territorial holdings; the islands of the South China Sea are a twenty-first-century version of Alsace-Lorraine, or Danzig.

Missing from both of these attempts to recast China's actions into more familiar ground is the role of sovereignty in the Chinese conception of its claims.

Beijing does not see its South China Sea activities in the same light as either nineteenth-century America or twentieth-century Germany. In protesting the entry of the USS *Lassen* into the waters near the artificial island China has built atop Subi Reef, the Chinese used language that makes their concerns quite clear. Foreign Ministry spokesperson Lu Kang declared that the USS *Lassen* "illegally entered waters near relevant islands and reefs of China's Nansha Islands without the permission of the Chinese government." He added that Beijing "has stressed on many occasions that China has indisputable sovereignty over the Nansha Islands and their adjacent waters. China's sovereignty and relevant rights over the South China Sea have been formed over the long course of history."

Sovereignty as the Central Issue

The Chinese formulation underscores that, from Beijing's perspective, the central issue is a basic one of sovereignty and territorial integrity. Chinese leadership since at least Deng Xiaoping has consistently characterized its approach to various maritime disputes in the same way: "Sovereignty is ours; defer disputes; engage in joint development." When Deng set forth this formulation in the 1980s, the emphasis was on the second two clauses. At the time, he suggested that this issue could be set aside for the next—and perhaps wiser—generation to resolve. In the meantime, China was open to joint exploitation of resources.

But where the emphasis under Deng was on rapidly pushing economic development, the focus under Hu Jintao, and even more under Xi Jinping, has steadily shifted to the first clause: "sovereignty is ours." Part of this shift is likely rooted in the UN Convention on the Law of the Sea (UNCLOS). UNCLOS required states to file formal declarations of their baselines by May 2009, or else risk losing their rights to seabed and offshore resources. As the various parties to the Spratlys dispute (including not only the PRC and Taiwan, but also Brunei, Malaysia, the Philippines and Vietnam) all had economic interests, it behooved them to file formal claims—claims which Beijing sees as jeopardizing its own claims to sovereignty.

But China's posture as the aggrieved party is not solely rooted in UNCLOS filings. One striking theme that arises in any discussion with Chinese officials regarding the South China Sea is the view that the neighboring states have been encroaching on China's territories—deliberately. Some of this, as General Fang Fenghui indicated when he visited the United States, is seen as inspired by American encouragement. But as important is the argument that China's neighbors are exploiting Beijing's patience and forbearance. Chinese interlocutors note that China has not drilled as many wells, has not built airfields and did not first expand its islands. The Chinese position is that they have shown restraint in not reacting to these activities—even though they are presumably occurring on Chinese territory.

This is the crux of the matter. For Chinese decision makers, the South China Sea—both the waters and the islands within it—are and have always been Chinese territory. The neighbors' actions are not merely alternative claims; they are an effort to amputate a piece of China. In this context, China is not Germany: China is France or Poland.

The same reasoning means that China is not intent upon establishing a sphere of influence over the South China Sea, in a modern version of the Monroe Doctrine. The United States dominated the Gulf of Mexico and Central America, but made no claim that Haiti or Guatemala was part of the United States itself. China, on the other hand, has made clear in its behavior, if not in its enunciated policies, that it views the waters and islands of the South China Sea as part of its sovereign territory. Hence, Chinese construction of artificial islands is perfectly within its rights, since it occurs within Chinese territory; China has no more need to consult with others over such construction than they would if they were building a new expressway in Beijing.

Sovereignty as a Core Interest

The situation is further exacerbated by the overall Chinese attitude toward sovereignty. There is probably no greater supporter of the Westphalian system of nation-states, and the attendant adherence to the sanctity of borders, than the PRC. It is the basis for China's claims to not only the South China Sea, but Taiwan, Xinjiang and Tibet. Given the Chinese experience with the "century of humiliation," when China confronted the real potential of dismemberment by the colonial powers, such a perspective should not be surprising.

Consequently, China views sovereignty, along with territorial integrity, as a "core interest." Dai Bingguo, then State Councilor for Foreign Affairs, stated in 2009 that for China, core interests are those that touch upon how the state is governed: i.e., the continued rule of the Chinese Communist Party, issues of territorial integrity and national sovereignty, and the ability of the PRC to develop its economy and society. Some Chinese and American analysts question whether the Chinese specifically used the term "core interest" in connection with the South China Sea, but China's behavior suggests that it views the region as, in fact, a core interest.

> In essence, China is challenging the international order, not by seeking "a place in the sun" or lebensraum, but by redefining and extending the reach of the state.

This view is unlikely to change for the foreseeable future. Indeed, China's growing military capability would suggest the exact opposite. In the 1980s and 1990s, China's military power was exceedingly limited; at the time, it was said that China had the world's best obsolete equipment. In that context, it was not in China's interest to press sovereignty claims even in the "near seas," as its air and naval forces were largely limited to coastal operations.

Today, however, China's military is a far more substantial force. The People's Liberation Army Navy (PLAN) easily outmatches any navy in Southeast Asia, especially among the rival claimants. Moreover, it can count upon the People's Liberation Army Air Force (PLAAF) and the Second Artillery to support it in any "near seas" or even "far seas" operations. The PRC is therefore far more able to uphold its sovereignty claims than in the past.

At the same time, its interest in the South China Sea has assumed even more of a security aspect. Hainan Island, an undisputed part of China, is rapidly becoming one of the most heavily militarized locations in China. It already hosts a carrier berth and submarine pens for China's seagoing nuclear deterrent and its attack submarines. It is also the home of China's newest spaceport, and multiple airbases are located there as well. China has a clear interest in keeping foreign interlopers out of the adjoining South China Sea.

An Expansive View of Sovereignty

This Chinese perspective on its sovereign rights over the South China Sea, of course, poses a real challenge for not only China's neighbors but the United States. While China believes that its historical claims justify its view that the entire South China Sea is Chinese territory, this ignores the claims of other states whose people have traversed its waters and used its islands for extended historical periods as well. Just as important, it fundamentally contradicts the principle of freedom of the seas. Some $5.3 trillion in commerce travels these sea lanes annually, heightening the potential global impact of China's claims.

But the problem goes beyond the waters encompassed within the so-called 9-dash line (now 10 dashes). Just as the South China Sea is not only about some reefs and spits of land, China's approach to sovereignty affects more than just that body of water. Beijing's increasing assertiveness in declaring various territories as actually part of China is mirrored by its attitudes toward other global common spaces.

Thus, China has undertaken a sustained effort to establish sovereignty in cyberspace, as it has sought to shift Internet governance to the International Telecommunications Union (ITU), where only nation-states are represented. Chinese officials claim that censorship of the Internet is perfectly justified, since it is up to each state to administer the Internet within its borders. Along similar lines, Chinese leaders such as Hu Jintao and Xi Jinping have both sounded the tocsin about the need to defend Chinese "cultural security" from foreign encroachment. This position was codified in the new PRC National Security Law, where it is noted that the state has a responsibility for cultural security.

In short, China is intent upon defining its sovereignty in extraordinarily expansive terms, not only in the area of the South China Sea, but across a variety of domains, both physical and virtual. These definitions contradict much of the current Western, and even global, understandings underpinning international commerce, whether it is freedom of the seas or the free flow of information. In essence, China is challenging the international order, not by seeking "a place in the sun" or *lebensraum*, but by redefining and extending the reach of the state.

The American response to this revisionism, both in the South China Sea and elsewhere, will therefore have far larger repercussions than just the immediate disputes. Beijing is waiting to see whether its efforts will be accepted or rebuffed. Just as importantly, it will mark the first step in determining whether Chinese or American principles will define the governance of global common spaces in the coming decades.

Print Citations

CMS: Cheng, Dean. "How China Views the South China Sea: A Sovereign Territory." In *The Reference Shelf: The South China Sea Conflict*, edited by Betsy Maury, 162-166. Ipswich, MA: H.W. Wilson, 2018.

MLA: Cheng, Dean. "How China Views the South China Sea: A Sovereign Territory." *The Reference Shelf: The South China Sea Conflict*. Ed. Betsy Maury. Ipswich: H.W. Wilson, 2018. 162-166. Print.

APA: Cheng, D. (2018). How China views the South China Sea: A sovereign territory. In Betsy Maury (Ed.), *The reference shelf: The South China Sea conflict* (pp. 162-166). Ipswich, MA: H.W. Wilson. (Original work published 2015)

Bibliography

Allard, Tom and Munthe, Bernadette Christina. "Asserting Sovereignty, Indonesia Renamed Part of South China Sea." *Reuters*. Reuters Inc. Jul 14 2017. Web. 16 Dec 2017.

"Arbitration between the Republic of the Philippines and the People's Republic of China." *PCA*. Permanent Court of Arbitration. Oct 29 2015. Web. 16 Dec 2017.

Beech, Hannah. "Just Where Exactly Did China Get the South China Sea Nine-Dash Line From?" *Time*. Time, Inc. Jul 19 2016. Web. 15 Nov 2017.

Benedict, Robert D. "The Historical Position of the Rhodian Law." *Yale Law Journal*. Vol. 18, No. 4. 1909, 223-42.

Bray, Adam. "The Cham: Descendants of Ancient Rulers of South China Sea Watch Maritime Dispute from Sidelines." *National Geographic*. National Geographic Society, LLC. Jun 18 2014. Web. 15 Dec 2017.

Bruckner, Andrew W. "Life-Saving Products from Coral Reefs." *Issues in Science and Technology*. Vol. 18, No. 3. 2002. Web. 18 Dec 2017.

Carroll, Clint. "Protecting the South China Sea: Chinese Island-Building and the Environment." *Foreign Affairs*. Council on Foreign Relations, Inc. Jun 9 2017. Web. 18 Dec 2017.

Caspersen, Nina. *Unrecognized States: The Struggle for Sovereignty in the Modern International System*. Malden, MA: Polity Press, 2012.

"China's Claims in the South China Sea." *The Wall Street Journal*. Dow Jones & Company. May 27 2015. Web. 16 Dec 2017.

"China's Maritime Disputes." *CFR*. Council on Foreign Relations. Jan 2017. Web. 16 Dec 2017.

Chinyong, Joseph. "Five Pillars for a US Strategy on the South China Sea." *The Straits Times*. Singapore Press Holdings Ltd. Co. Aug 1 2017. Web. 18 Dec 2017.

Crawford, James R. *The Creation of States in International Law (2nd ed)*. New York: Oxford University Press, 2007.

Croxton, Derek. "The Peace of Westphalia of 1648 and the Origins of Sovereignty." *The International History Review*. Vol. 21, No. 3 (Sep. 1999), 569.

Daiss, Tim. "Newly Found Maps Dispute Beijing's South China Sea Claims." *Forbes*. Forbes, Inc. Jun 1 2016. Web. 16 Dec 2017.

Dennis, Brady, Juliet Eilperin, and Chris Mooney. "Trump Administration Releases Report Finding 'No Convincing Alternative Explanation' for Climate Change." *The Washington Post*. The Washington Post Company. Nov 3 2017. Web. 18 Dec 2017.

Drifte, Reinhard. "Japan's Policy towards the South China Sea—Applying 'Proactive Peace Diplomacy'?" *PRIF.* Peace Research Institute Frankfurt. 2016. Web. 16 Dec 2017.

"Factbox: What Trump Has Said about the United Nations." *Reuters.* Reuters. Sep 17 2017. Web. 16 Nov 2017.

"Global Greenhouse Gas Emissions Data." *EPA.* Environmental Protection Agency. 2015. Web. 18 Dec 2017.

Goldstein, Lyle J. *Meeting China Halfway: How to Defuse the Emerging US-China Rivalry.* Washington, DC: Georgetown University Press, 2015.

"History of the United Nations." *UN.* United Nations. 2016. Web. 16 Nov 2017.

Hodges, Doyle. "Back to Basics in the South China Sea." *Lawfare.* The Lawfare Institute. Apr 13 2016. Web. 15 Nov 2017.

"How Much Trade Transits the South China Sea?" *China Power.* Center for Strategic & International Studies. Aug 2 2017. Web. 15 Dec 2017.

Hutt, David. "Malaysia Speaks Softly in the South China Sea." *Asia Times.* Asia Times Holding Limited. Mar 23 2017. Web. 16 Dec 2017.

Jennings, Ralph. "South China Sea Succumbing to Pollution Due to Political Impasse." *VOA.* VOA News. Sep 12 2017. Web. 18 Dec 2017.

Jiang, Steven and Kevin Bohn. "China Returns Seized US Underwater Drone." *CNN.* CNN Politics. Dec 20 2016. Web. 19 Dec 2017.

Jozuka, Emiko. "Japan to Join US in South China Sea Patrols." *CNN.* CNN. Sep 16 2016. Web. 16 Dec 2017.

Kontorovich, Eugene. "Arctic Sunrise (Netherlands v. Russia)." *The American Journal of International Law.* Vol. 110, No. 1 (January 2016), 96-102.

Ku, Julian. "Why the U.S. Can't Take Sides in South China Sea Sovereignty Disputes, Even against China." *Lawfare.* Lawfare Institute. Jun 19 2017. Web. 18 Dec 2017.

LaGrone, Sam. "Chine Chides U.S. over Latest South China Sea Freedom of Navigation Operation." *USNI.* U.S. Naval Institute. Oct 11 2017. Web. 18 Dec 2017.

Lee, YingHui. "A South China Sea Code of Conduct: Is Real Progress Possible?" *The Diplomat.* Nov 18 2017. Web. 18 Dec 2017.

Levins, Nicole. "Coral Reefs Could Hold the Cures for Some of the Human Race's Most Common—and Serious—Ailments." *Nature.* Nature Conservancy. 2017. Web. 18 Dec 2017.

Liu, J.Y. "Status of Marine Biodiversity of the China Seas." *PLoS ONE.* Jan 8 2013. Web. 18 Dec 2017.

Makinen, Julie. "China Has Been Killing Turtles, Coral and Giant Clams in the South China Sea, Tribunal Finds." *Los Angeles Times.* Jul 13 2016. Web. 18 Dec 2017.

Manning, Robert A. and James Przystup. "Stop the South China Sea Charade." *Foreign Policy.* FP Group. Aug 17 2017. Web. 17 Dec 2017.

Mourdoukoutas, Panos. "In The South China Sea, Duterte's Playing China against America and Japan—Nicely." *Forbes.* Forbes, Inc. Nov 3 2017. Web. 16 Dec 2017.

"Oil and Gas: Top Recipients." *Opensecrets*. Center for Responsive Politics. 2017. Web. 18 Dec 2017.

Pedrozo, Raul. "China versus Vietnam: An Analysis of the Competing Claims in the South China Sea." *CNA Corporation*. CNA. Aug 2014. Web. 16 Dec 2017.

Pesek, William. "Making Sense of the South China Sea Dispute." *Forbes*. Forbes Inc. Aug 22 2017. Web. 18 Dec 2017.

Pham, Nga. "Shift as Vietnam Marks South China Sea Battle." *BBC*. BBC News. Jan 15 2014. Web. 15 Nov 2017.

Roach, J. Ashley. "Malaysia and Brunei: An Analysis of Their Claims in the South China Sea." *CNA Corporation*. Aug 2014. Web. 16 Dec 2017.

Rosen, Mark E. "Philippine Claims in the South China Sea: A Legal Analysis." *CNA Corporation*. CNA. Aug 2014. Web. 16 Dec 2017.

Shen, Dingli. "Why China Has the Right to 'Build Sovereignty' in the South China Sea." *Huffington Post*. The World Post. 2017. Web. 18 Dec 2017.

Shenon, Philip. "Manila Sees China Threat on Coral Reef." *The New York Times*. The New York Times Co. Feb 19 1995. Web. 15 Nov 2017.

"A Short History of The Hague." *Denhaag*. The Hague. 2016. Web. 15 Nov 2017.

Smith, Robert S. "Recent Criticism of the Consulate of the Sea." *The Hispanic American Historical Review*. Vol. 14, No. 3 (Aug 1934), 359-63.

"South China Sea, between the Philippines, Borneo, Vietnam, and China." *Worldwildlife*. World Wildlife Fund. 2017. Web. 18 Dec 2017.

"South China Sea Countries to Cooperate on Integrating Fisheries and Marine Ecosystem Management." *UNEP*. United Nations Environment. Nov 1 2016. Web. 18 Dec 2017.

"Sovereignty." *Plato.stanford*. Stanford Encyclopedia of Philosophy. Mar 25 2016. Web. 18 Dec 2017.

Standifer, Cid. "UPDATED: A Brief History of U.S. Freedom of Navigation Operations in the South China Sea." *USNI*. US Naval Institute. Jul 2 2017. Web. 18 Dec 2017.

Sterling, Joe. "US Destroyer in South China Sea Called 'Provocation' by Beijing." *CNN*. CNN Politics. Aug 10 2017. Web. 18 Dec 2017.

Thomas, Madeleine. "Climate Depression Is for Real: Just Ask a Scientist." *Grist*. Grist Magazine Inc. Oct 28 2014. Web. 18 Dec 2017.

Torode, Greg. "'Paving Paradise': Scientists Alarmed over China Island Building in Disputed Sea." *Reuters*. Reuters Inc. Jun 25 2015. Web. 18 Dec 2017.

"UN Documentation: International Law." *UN*. United Nations Dag Hammarskjöld Library. Nov 2017. Web. 18 Dec 2017.

"United Nations Convention on the Law of the Sea." *UN*. United Nations. May 4 2017. Web. 16 Nov 2017.

"U.S. Department of Defense Freedom of Navigation Program." *DOD*. Department of Defense. Mar 2015. Web. 18 Dec 2017.

Valencia, Mark J. "Are US FONOPs in the South China Sea Necessary?" *The Diplomat*. The Diplomat. Oct 28 2017. Web. 18 Dec 2017.

Vuving, Alexander L. "How America Can Take Control in the South China Sea." *Foreign Policy*. Foreign Policy Institute, Inc. Feb 13 2017. Web. 18 Dec 2017.

Wang, Jennifer. "Trump's Stock Portfolio: Big Oil, Big Banks and More Foreign Connections." *Forbes*. Forbes Inc. Nov 29 2016. Web. 18 Dec 2017.

Wan, William. "In South China Sea, Every Side Has Its Say." *The Washington Post*. The Washington Post Co. Jun 20 2011. Web. 15 Nov 2017.

———. "Panetta, in Speech in Singapore, Seeks to Lend Heft to U.S. Pivot to Asia." *The Washington Post*. The Washington Post, Co. Jun 1 2012. Web. 15 Nov 2017.

"Why Is the South China Sea Contentious?" *BBC*. BBC News. Jul 12 2016. Web. 16 Nov 2017.

Zhang, Y.H., G. Qin, X. Wang, and Q. Lin. "A New Species of Seahorse (*Teleostei: Syngnathidae*) from the South China Sea." *Zootaxa*. Sep 23, 2016. Web. 18 Dec 2017.

Websites

Association of Southeast Asian States (ASEAN)

www.asean.org
The Association of Southeast Asian Nations, established in 1967, is a regional governmental organization that seeks to establish intergovernmental cooperation between southeast Asian states. The group has 10 member states—Brunei, Cambodia, Indonesia, Laos, Malaysia, Myanmar, the Philippines, Singapore, Thailand, and Vietnam, but regularly conducts summits with neighboring Asian nations including Bangladesh, China, and India.

United Nations (UN)

www.un.org
The United Nations is an international governmental group founded after World War II in an effort to avoid global conflict and to promote intergovernmental cooperation and partnerships towards collective goals. Founded in 1945, the United Nations has 193 member countries and is headquartered in New York City. The United Nations has also created a system of international law organized through a series of courts and tribunals located in the Hague, including the Permanent Court of Arbitration (PCA) and the International Criminal Court (ICC).

Division for Ocean Affairs and the Law of the Sea

www.un.org/depts/los
The United Nation's Division for Ocean Affairs and the Law of the Sea is a multinational UN group dedicated to developing, implementing, and enforcing international agreements regarding the ownership and use of oceanic territory. The United Nations Convention on the Law of the Sea is an international agreement resulting from the third UNCLOS conference and representing the most recent international law regarding maritime territory. UNCLOS has 168 member countries, 157 signatories, and 60 ratifications from member countries.

Ministry of Foreign Affairs of the People's Republic of China

www.fmprc.gov
The People Republic of China's Ministry of Foreign Affairs is the branch of the Chinese government responsible for formulating policies and releasing statements on the nation's diplomatic and international issues. The Chinese Ministry of Foreign Affairs released numerous statements and policy announcements with regard to the nation's territorial program in the South China Sea.

Limits in the Seas

www.state.gov/e/oes/ocns/opa/c16065.htm

The Limits in the Seas collection, from the U.S. Department of State, includes a series of documents dating from 1970 to 2014 detailing US and related foreign policy regarding maritime territory. The studies included represent the perspective of the United States government and have been used to determine US policy with regard to ASEAN and Chinese claims to South China Sea islands and reefs.

Council of Foreign Relations (CFR)

www.cfr.org

The Council of Foreign Relations is a US-based non-profit think tank specializing in foreign policy and foreign affairs. Founded in 1921, the CFR invites commentary and involvement from politicians, intelligence industry specialists, banking, law, and academic professionals and creates studies on key international issues. The CFR has published studies and press released on the ongoing South China Sea conflict between 2015 and 2018.

CNA Corporation

www.cna.org

The CNA Corporation is a nonprofit think tank and research organization headquartered in Arlington, Virginia, and specializing in naval policy. Since 2015, CNA has been commissioned to produce several detailed reports detailing the historic, environmental, military, and cultural claims to the islands and reefs of the South China Sea.

The South China Sea

www.southchinasea.org

Southchinasea.org is a website created, edited, and maintained by political science professor David Rosenberg of Middlebury College, first launched in 1999. The website contains a wealth of resources for students, journalists, and scholars interested in the various issues surrounding the South China Sea controversy between 1999 and 2000. The southchinasea.org website also contains links to research reports, governmental press releases, and organizations involved in various aspects of the controversy.

Index